Swindon Chippenham, Devizes & Marlborough

Blunsdon St. Andrew	1	Marlborough	27
Broad Blunsdon	2	Moredon	5
Calne	29	New & Old Town	12
Chippenham	21	Nine Elms	10
Chiseldon	20	North Tidworth	36
Corsham	35	North Wroughton	18
Covingham	14	Okus	12
Cricklade	30	Peatmoor	4
Devizes	25	Penhill	6
Eldene	14	Pewsey	34
Even Swindon	11	Purton	3
Freshbrook	10	Rodbourne	6
Gorse Hill	6	Roughmoor	4
Grange Park	10	Shaw	10
Greenmeadow	6	South Marston	8
Haydon Wick	5	Sparcells	5
Highworth	31	Stratton St. Margaret	7
Hyde	7	Swindon Centre	37
Kingshill	12	Walcot, East & West	13
Liden	20	Westlea	11
Lydiard Millicent	9	Woodshaw	15
Lyneham	34	Wootton Bassett	33
Malmesbury	32	Wroughton	17

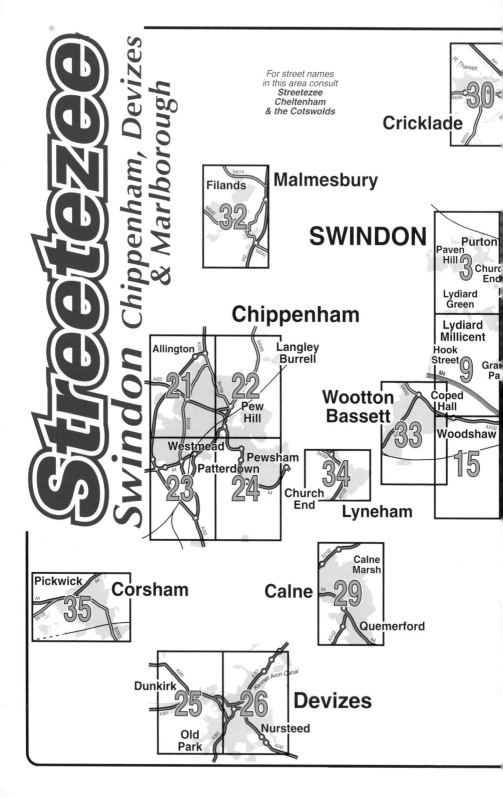

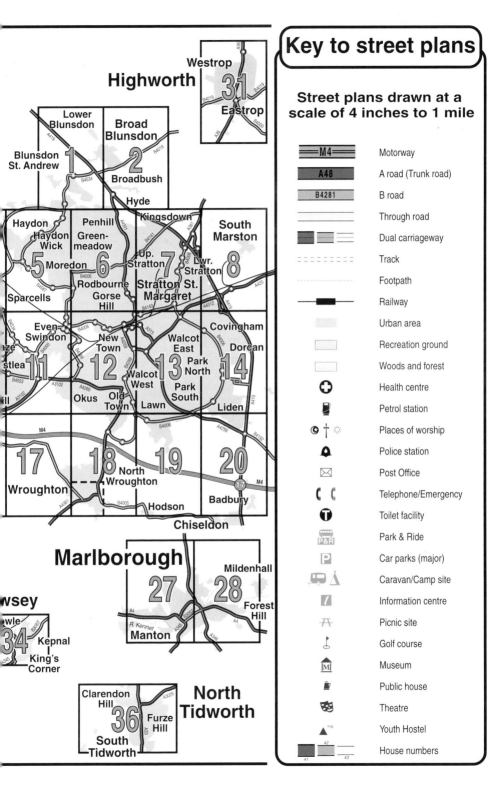

Key to street plans

Street plans drawn at a scale of 4 inches to 1 mile

M4	Motorway
A48	A road (Trunk road)
B4281	B road
———	Through road
▬▬ ▬▬ ═══	Dual carriageway
– – – – –	Track
·········	Footpath
■▬■	Railway
▨	Urban area
▭	Recreation ground
▭	Woods and forest
✚	Health centre
▮	Petrol station
☪ † ✡	Places of worship
♤	Police station
⊠	Post Office
((	Telephone/Emergency
⊺	Toilet facility
P&R	Park & Ride
P	Car parks (major)
🚐 ⛺	Caravan/Camp site
i	Information centre
🛆	Picnic site
⚑	Golf course
M	Museum
▮	Public house
🎭	Theatre
▲ YHA	Youth Hostel
41 42 43	House numbers

Highworth

Westrop
31
Eastrop

Lower Blunsdon
Broad Blunsdon
1 Blunsdon St. Andrew
2 Broadbush
Hyde

Haydon / Haydon Wick
Penhill / Green-meadow
Kingsdown
South Marston
5 Moredon
6 Rodbourne / Gorse Hill
7 Up. Stratton / Stratton St. Margaret / Lwr. Stratton
8
Sparcells

Even-Swindon
Covingham
Dorcan
11 / **12** New Town / Walcot West / Okus / Old Town
13 Walcot East / Park North / Park South / Lawn
14 Liden
stlea

17 Wroughton
18 North Wroughton / Hodson
19
20 Badbury
Chiseldon

Marlborough

Mildenhall
27 / **28** Manton / R. Kennet
Forest Hill

wsey
34 Kepnal / King's Corner
wle

Clarendon Hill
36 Furze Hill
South Tidworth
North Tidworth

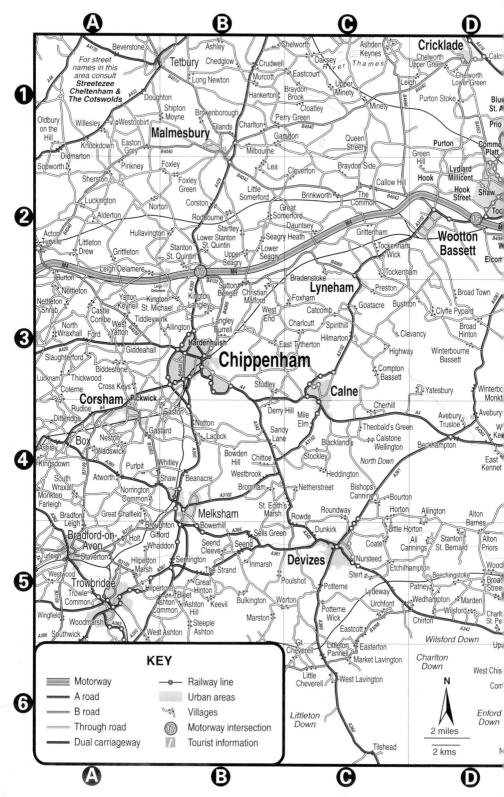

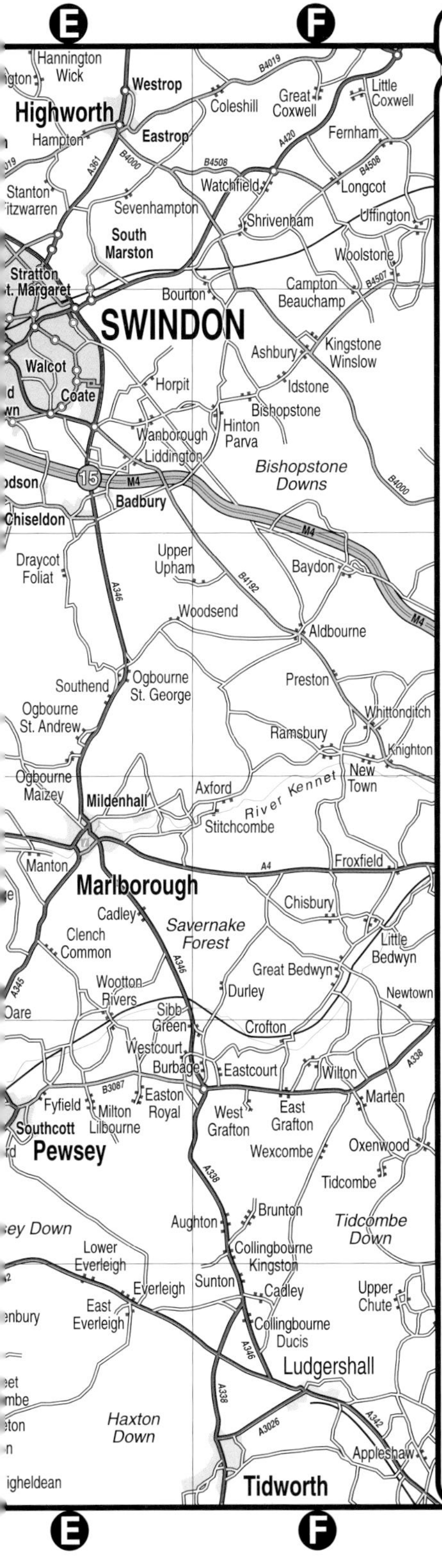

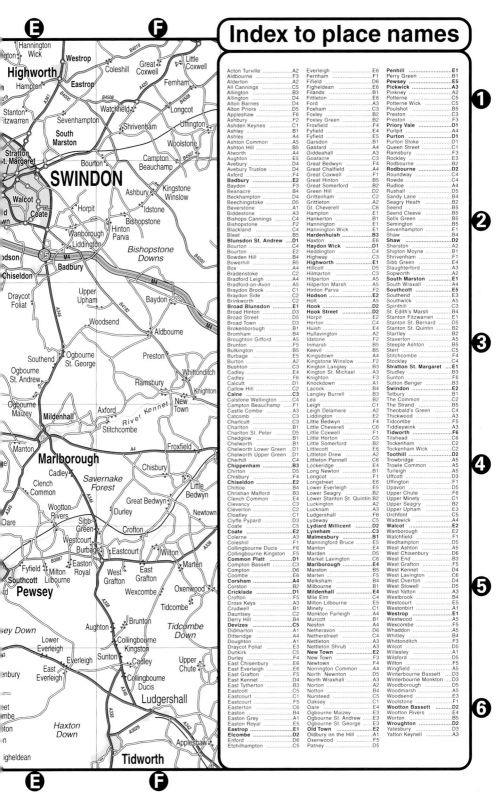

Index to place names

Acton Turville A2
Aldbourne F3
Alderton A2
All Cannings C5
Allington B3
Allington D4
Alton Barnes D4
Alton Priors D5
Appleshaw F6
Ashbury F2
Ashden Keynes C1
Ashley B1
Ashley A4
Ashton Common A5
Ashton Hill B5
Atworth A4
Aughton E5
Avebury D4
Avebury Trusloe D4
Axford F4
Badbury E2
Baydon F3
Beanacre B4
Beckhampton D4
Beechingstoke D5
Beverstone A1
Biddestone A3
Bishops Cannings C4
Bishopstone F2
Blackland C4
Bleet B5
Blunsdon St. Andrew D1
Bourton C4
Bourton E2
Bowden Hill B4
Bowerhill B5
Box A4
Bradenstoke C2
Bradford Leigh A4
Bradford-on-Avon A5
Braydon Brook C1
Braydon Side C2
Brinkworth C2
Broad Blunsdon E1
Broad Hinton D3
Broad Street D5
Broad Town D3
Brokenborough B1
Bromham B4
Broughton Gifford A5
Brunton F5
Bulkington B5
Burbage E5
Burton A2
Bushton C3
Cadley E4
Cadley F6
Calcutt D1
Callow Hill C2
Calne C3
Calstone Wellington C4
Campton Beauchamp F1
Castle Combe A3
Catcomb C3
Charlcutt C3
Charlton B1
Charlton St. Peter D5
Chedglow B1
Chelworth B1
Chelworth Lower Green D1
Chelworth Upper Green D1
Cherhill C4
Chippenham B3
Chirton D5
Chisbury F4
Chiseldon E2
Chittoe B4
Christian Malford B3
Clench Common E4
Clevancy C3
Cleverton C2
Cloatley C1
Clyffe Pypard D3
Coate C5
Coate E2
Colerne A3
Coleshill F1
Collingbourne Ducis F6
Collingbourne Kingston F5
Common Platt D1
Compton Bassett C3
Compton D6
Coombe E6
Corsham A4
Corston B2
Cricklade D1
Crofton F5
Cross Keys A3
Crudwell B1
Dauntsey C2
Derry Hill B4
Devizes C5
Didmarton A1
Ditteridge A4
Doughton A1
Draycot Foliat E3
Dunkirk C5
Durley F4
East Chisenbury E6
East Everleigh E6
East Grafton F5
East Kennet D4
East Tytherton B3
Eastcott C5
Eastcourt C1
Eastcourt F5
Easterton C6
Easton B4
Easton Grey A1
Easton Royal E5
Eastrop E1
Elcombe D2
Enford D6
Etchilhampton C5
Everleigh E6
Fernham F1
Fifield D6
Figheldean E6
Filands B1
Fittleton E6
Ford A3
Foxham C3
Foxley B2
Foxley Green B2
Froxfield F4
Fyfield E4
Fyfield E5
Garsdon B1
Gastard A4
Giddeahall A3
Goatacre C3
Great Bedwyn F4
Great Chalfield A4
Great Coxwell F1
Great Hinton B5
Great Somerford B2
Green Hill D2
Grittenham C2
Grittleton A2
Gt. Cheverell C6
Hampton E1
Hankerton B1
Hannington E1
Hannington Wick E1
Hardenhuish B3
Haxton E6
Haydon Wick D1
Heddington C4
Highway C3
Highworth E1
Hillcott D5
Hilmarton C3
Hilperton A5
Hilperton Marsh A5
Hinton Parva F2
Hodson E2
Holt A5
Hook D2
Hook Street D2
Horpit E2
Horton C4
Huish E4
Hullavington A2
Idstone F2
Inmarsh B5
Keevil B5
Kingsdown A4
Kingstone Winslow F2
Kington Langley B3
Kington St. Michael A3
Knighton F3
Knockdown A1
Lacock B4
Langley Burrell B3
Lea B2
Leigh C1
Leigh Delamere A2
Liddington E2
Little Bedwyn F4
Little Cheverell C6
Little Coxwell F1
Little Horton C5
Little Somerford B2
Littlecott E6
Littleton Drew A2
Littleton Pannell C6
Lockeridge E4
Long Newton B1
Longcot F1
Longstreet E6
Lower Everleigh E5
Lower Seagry B2
Lower Stanton St. Quintin B2
Luckington A2
Lucknam A3
Ludgershall F6
Lydeway C5
Lydiard Millicent D2
Lyneham C3
Malmesbury B1
Manningford Bruce E5
Manton E4
Marden D5
Market Lavington C6
Marlborough E4
Marston B5
Marten F5
Melksham B4
Milbourne B1
Mildenhall E4
Mile Elm C4
Milton Lilbourne E5
Minety C1
Monkton Farleigh A4
Murcott B1
Neston A4
Netheravon D6
Netherstreet C4
Nettleton A3
Nettleton Shrub A3
New Town E2
New Town F3
Newtown F4
Norrington Common A4
North Newnton D5
North Wraxhall A3
Norton A2
Notton B4
Nursteed C5
Oaksey C1
Oare E4
Ogbourne Maizey E3
Ogbourne St. Andrew E3
Ogbourne St. George E3
Old Town E2
Oldbury on the Hill A1
Oxenwood F5
Patney D5
Penhill E1
Perry Green B1
Pewsey E5
Pickwick A3
Pinkney A2
Potterne C5
Potterne Wick C5
Poulshot B5
Preston C3
Preston F3
Priory Vale D1
Purlpit A4
Purton D1
Purton Stoke D1
Queen Street C1
Ramsbury F3
Rockley E3
Rodbourne B2
Rodbourne D2
Roundway C4
Rowde C4
Rudloe A4
Rushall D5
Sandy Lane B4
Seagry Heath B2
Seend B5
Seend Cleeve B5
Sells Green B5
Semington B5
Sevenhampton E1
Shaw B4
Shaw D2
Sherston A2
Shipton Moyne B1
Shrivenham F1
Sibb Green E4
Slaughterford A3
Sopworth A2
South Marston E1
South Wraxall A4
Southcott E5
Southend E3
Southwick A5
Spirithill C3
St. Edith's Marsh B4
Stanton Fitzwarren E1
Stanton St. Bernard D5
Stanton St. Quintin B2
Startley B2
Staverton A5
Steeple Ashton B5
Stert C5
Stitchcombe F4
Stockley C4
Stratton St. Margaret E1
Studley B3
Sunton F6
Sutton Benger B3
Swindon E2
Tetbury B1
The Common C2
The Strand B5
Theobald's Green C4
Thickwood A3
Tidcombe F5
Tiddleywink A3
Tidworth F6
Tilshead C6
Tockenham C2
Tockenham Wick C2
Toothill D2
Trowbridge A5
Trowle Common A5
Turleigh A5
Uffcott D3
Uffington F1
Upavon D5
Upper Chute F6
Upper Minety C1
Upper Seagry B2
Upper Upham E3
Urchfont C5
Wadswick A4
Walcot E2
Wanborough E2
Watchfield F1
Wedhampton D5
West Ashton A5
West Chisenbury D6
West End B3
West Grafton F5
West Kennet D4
West Lavington C6
West Overton D4
West Stowell D5
West Yatton A3
Westbrook B4
Westcourt E5
Westonbirt A1
Westrop E1
Westwood A5
Wexcombe F5
Whaddon A5
Whitley B4
Whittonditch F3
Wilcot D5
Willesley A1
Wilsford D5
Wilton F5
Wingfield A5
Winterbourne Bassett D3
Winterbourne Monkton D3
Woodborough D5
Woodmarsh A5
Woodsend E3
Woolstone F1
Wootton Bassett D2
Wootton Rivers E4
Worton B5
Wroughton D2
Yatesbury D3
Yatton Keynell A3

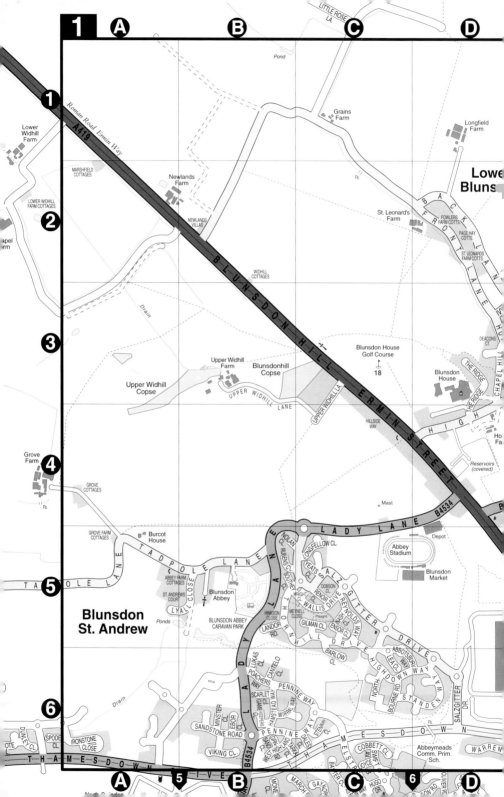

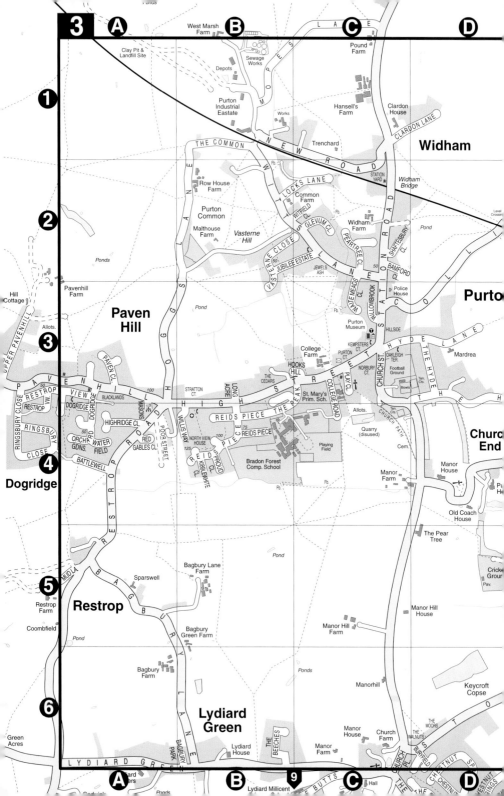

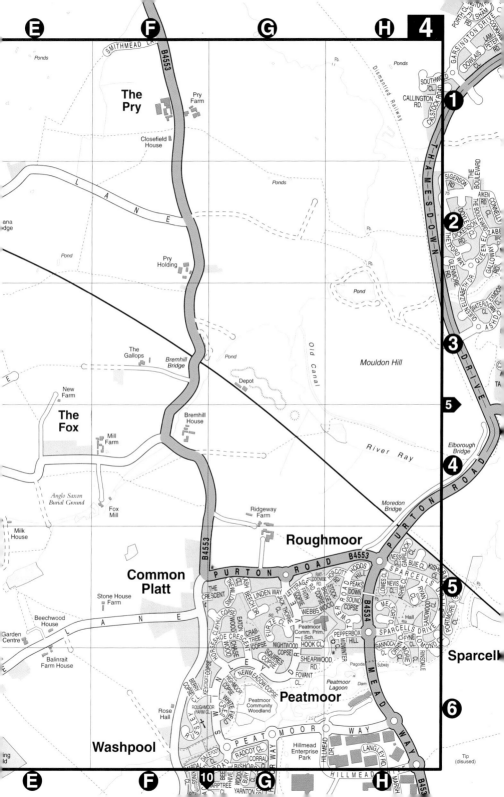

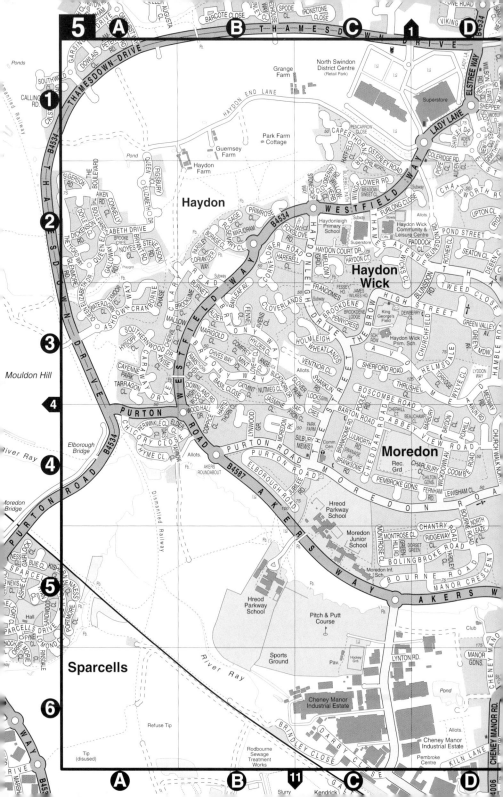

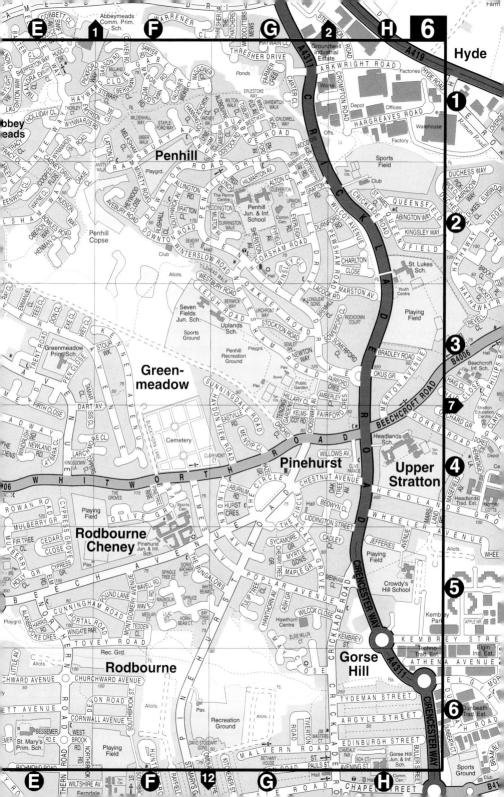

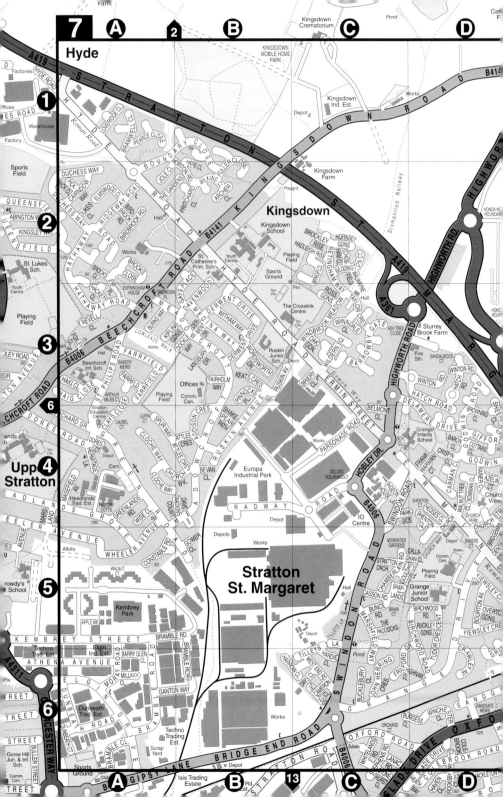

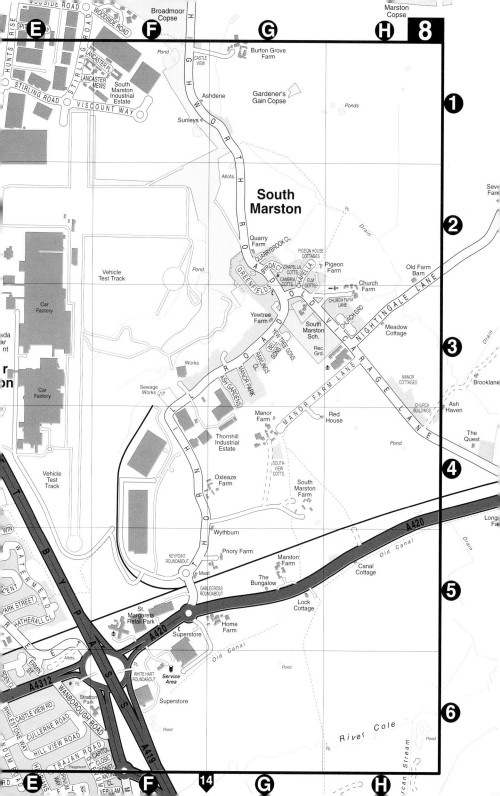

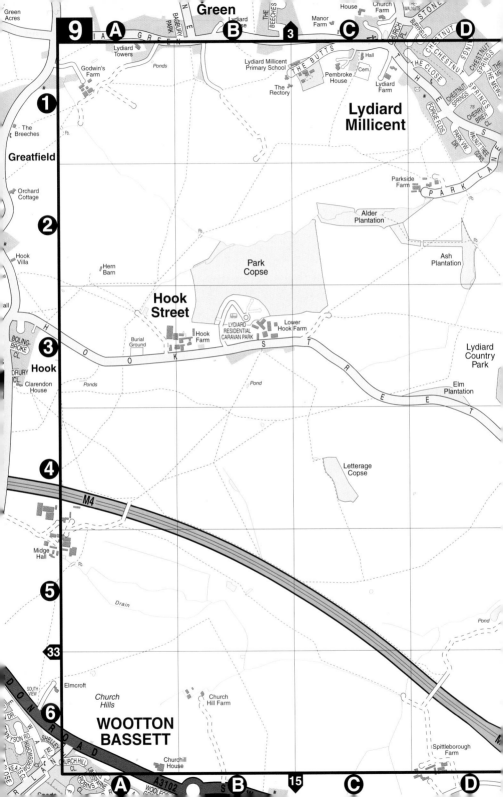

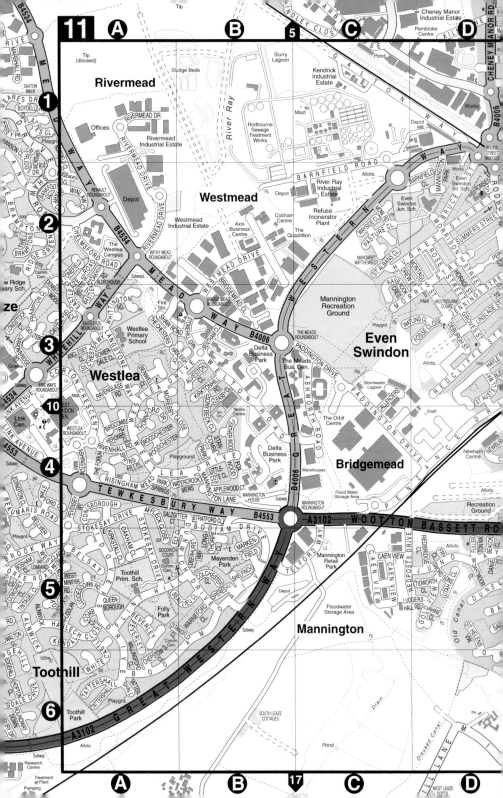

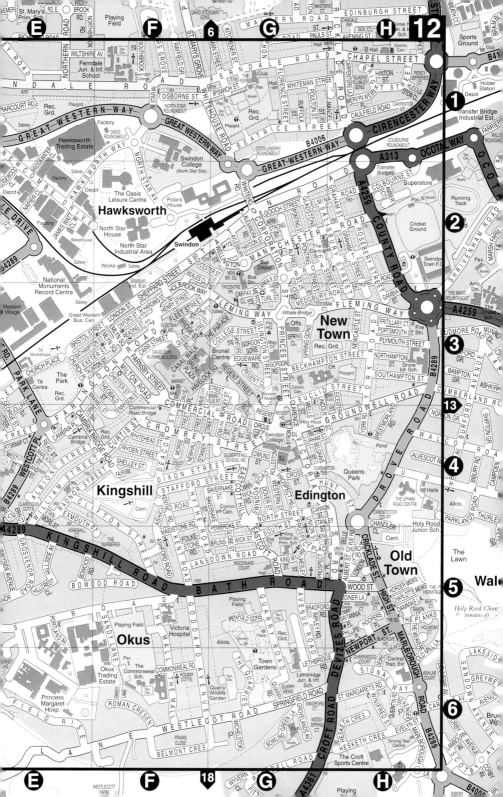

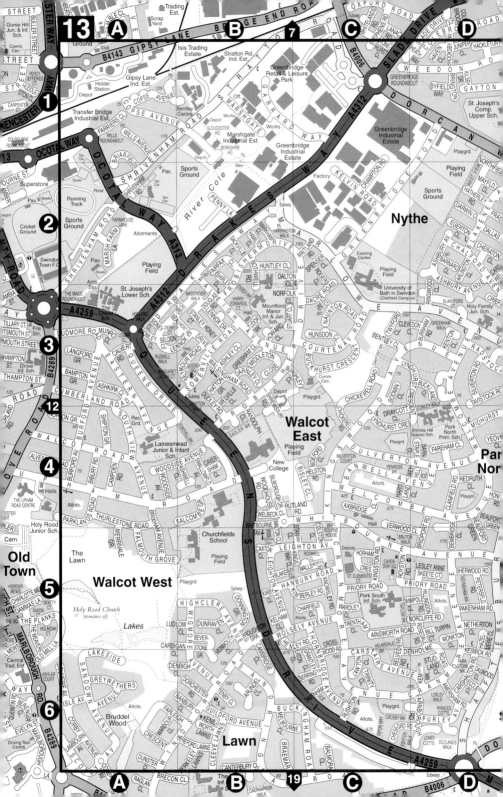

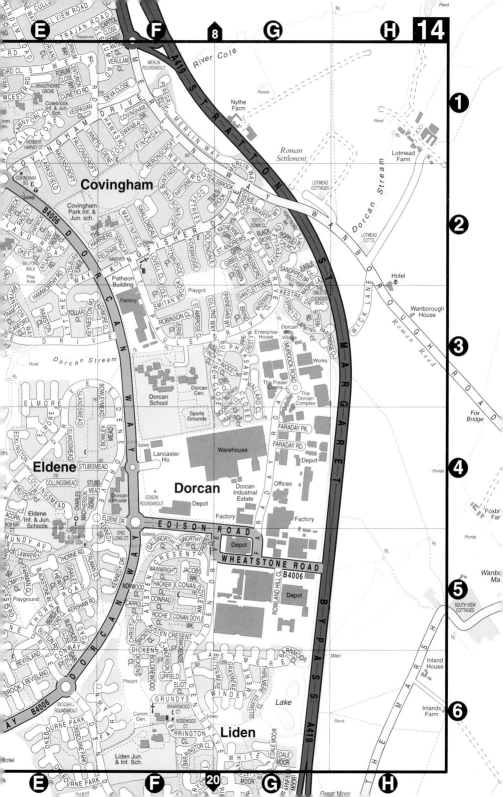

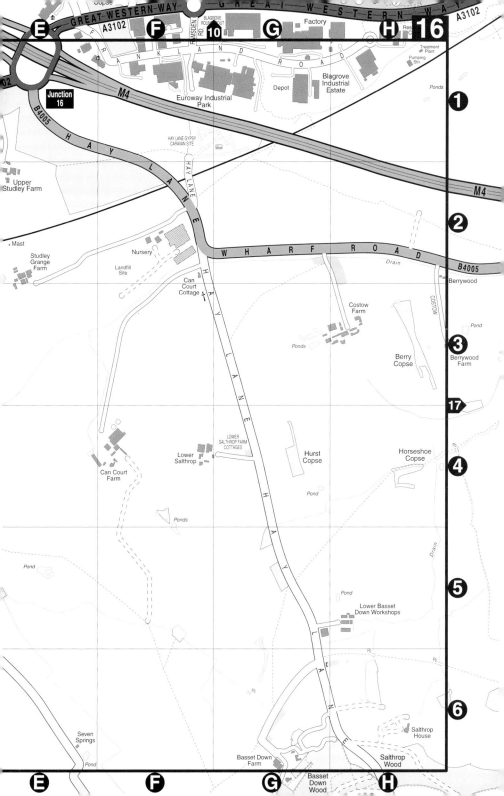

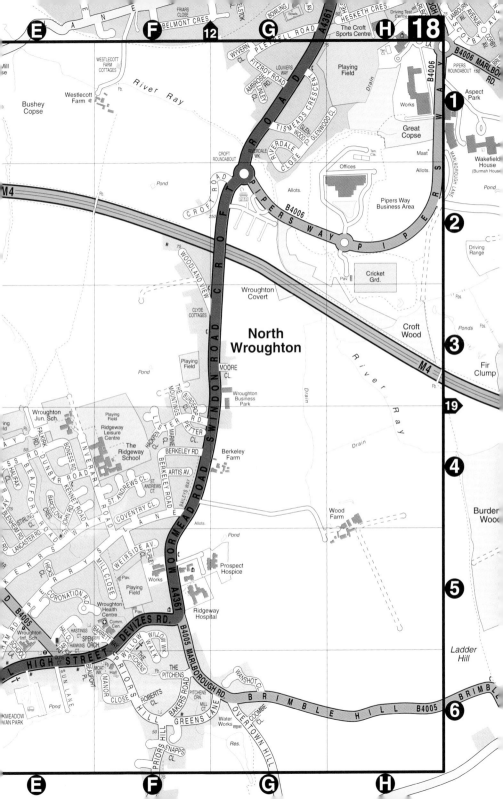

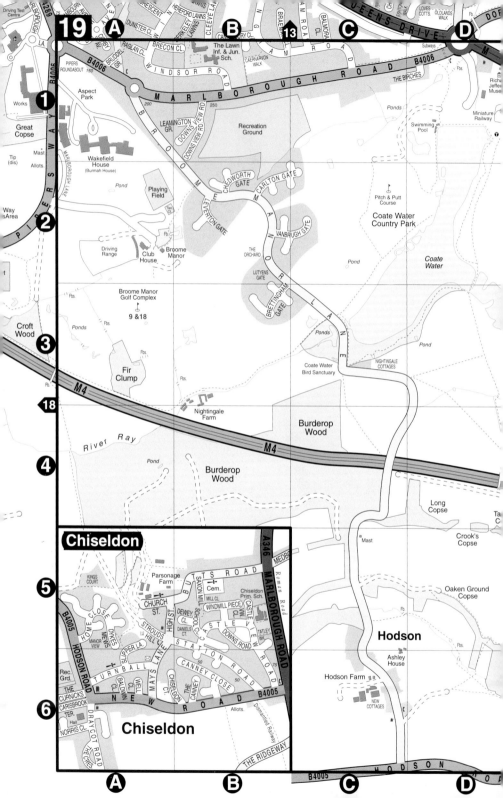

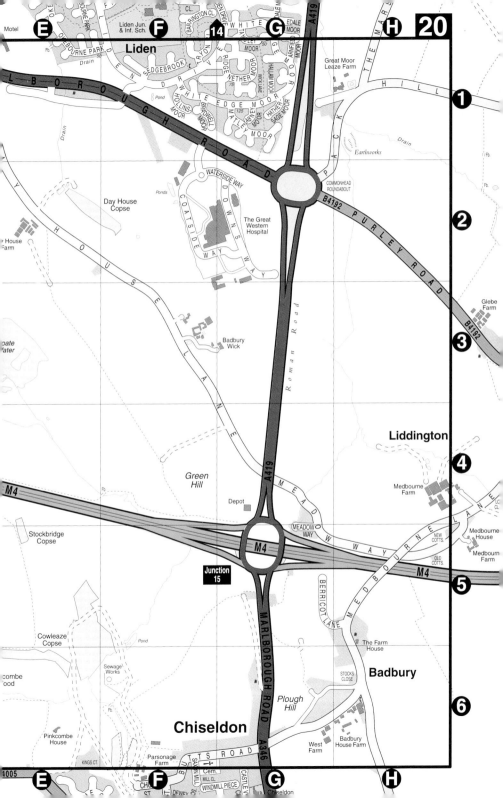

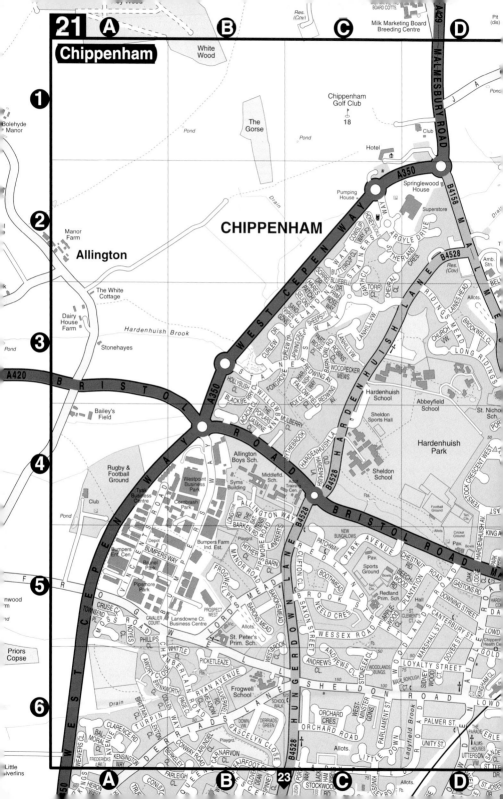

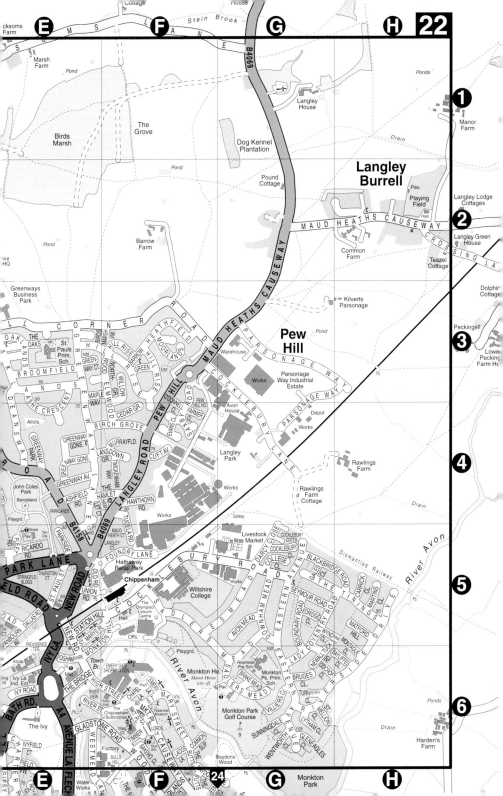

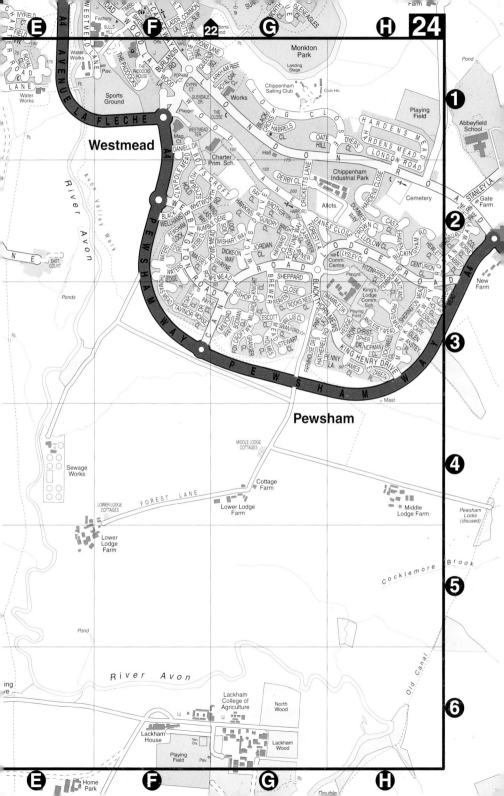

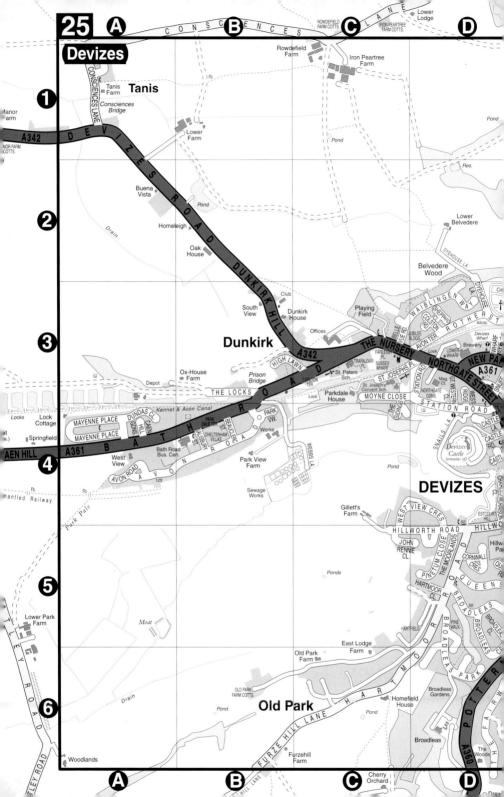

A · **B** · **C** · **D**

1 · **2** · **3** · **4** · **5** · **6**

CONSCIENCES

ROWDEFIELD FARM COTTS.

LANE

Lower Lodge

IRON PEARTREE FARM COTTS.

Rowdefield Farm

Iron Peartree Farm

Tanis Farm

Tanis

Consciences Bridge

CONSCIENCES LANE

Manor Farm

NOR FARM COTTS.

A342

DEVIZES

ROAD

Lower Farm

Pond

Pond

Res.

Buena Vista

Homeleigh

Pond

Lower Belvedere

Oak House

DUNKIRK HILL

Drain

DYEHOUSE LA.

Belvedere Wood

Club

South View

Dunkirk House

Dunkirk

Offices

A342

Playing Field

WAIBLINGEN WAY

SHEPPARD CL.

ROTHER

Devizes Wharf

Brewery

NEW PAR

A361

BELLE

FARLEIGH PL.

JUBILEE BLDGS.

JOE RD.

CRANSTON RD.

AVON TER.

NORTHGATE ST.

Ox-House Farm

HIGH LAWN

Depot

Prison Bridge

Lock

THE LOCKS

TRAFALGAR TER.

St. Peters Sch.

CARLTON TER.

SUSSEX WHARF

ST. JOSEPHS PL.

St. Joseph's Convent Sch.

Lower Wharf

Mag. Ct.

NORTHGATE GDNS.

STATION RD.

GT. WESTERN

RIDGE

WEST

STATION ROAD

THE SIDINGS

B A T H

R O A D

Parkdale House

St. Peters Sch.

MOYNE CLOSE

Locks

Lock Cottage

Springfield

AEN HILL

A361

MAYENNE PLACE

MAYENNE PLACE

DUNDAS CL.

CAEN HILL GDNS.

Kennet & Avon Canal

BENN CLERC

SALISBURY

PARK OAK TER.

CHELTENHAM VILLAS

PARK VW.

Works

THE SIDINGS

SNAILS LA.

CASTLE

CASTLE

Devizes Castle (remains of)

CASTLE

CASTLE RD.

West View

AVON ROAD

Bath Road Bus. Cen.

A V O N

R O A D

125

Park View Farm

WEBBS LA.

Pond

DEVIZES

antled Railway

Pb.

Pb.

Sewage Works

Gillett's Farm

WEST VIEW CRES.

ESTCOURT HILL

HILLWORTH ROAD

HILLW

Park Pale

JOHN RENNIE CL.

THE MOORLANDS

CORNWALL CRES.

Hillwo Pa

QUE

Ponds

PINETUM CLOSE

QUEENS

HARTMOOR CL.

PINE WALK

HARTFIELD

BROADLEAS

BROADLEAS

BROADLE

5

Lower Park Farm

Moat

LEY ROAD

East Lodge Farm

BROADLEAS PARK

50

POTTER

Old Park Farm

HARTMOOR

Homefield House

Pond

Broadleas Gardens

FAIR

A360

6

OLD PARK FARM COTTS.

Old Park

FURZE HILL LANE

Furzehill Farm

Broadleas

The Woods

Drain

Pond

Pond

Woodlands

Cherry Orchard

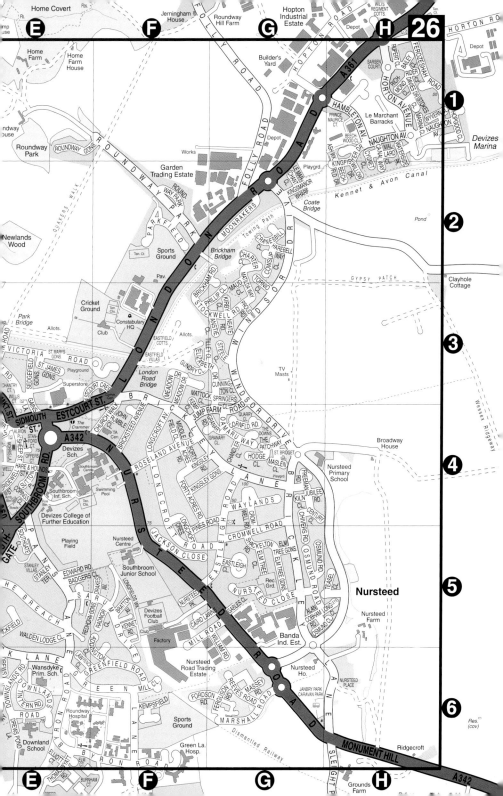

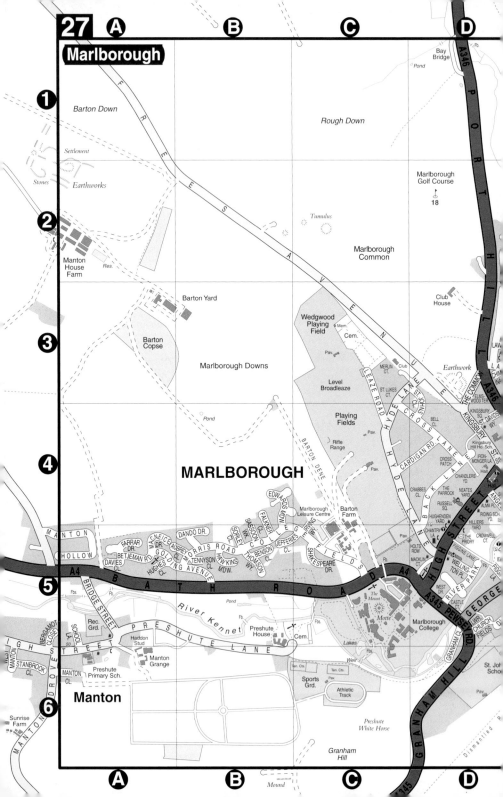

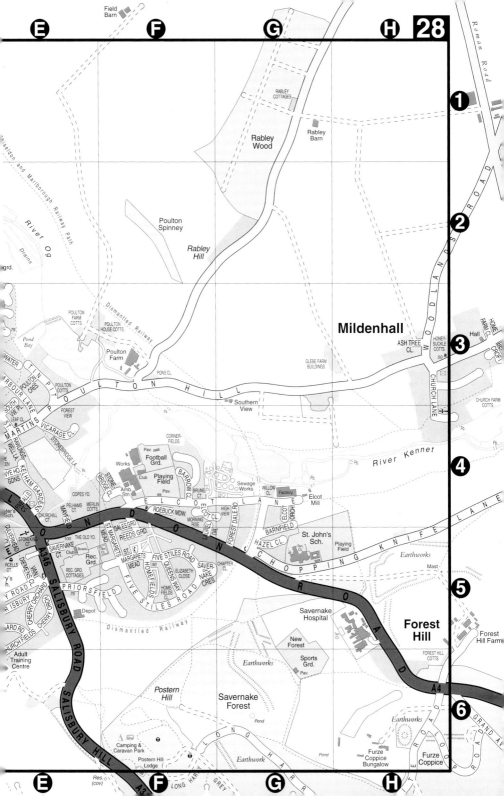

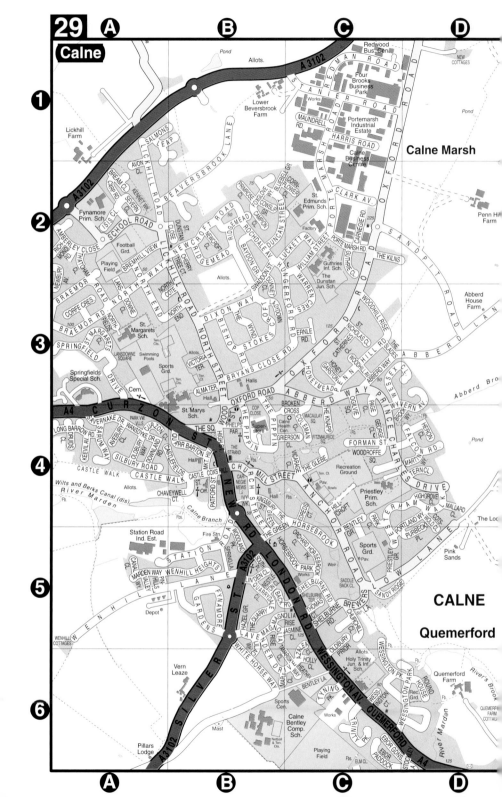

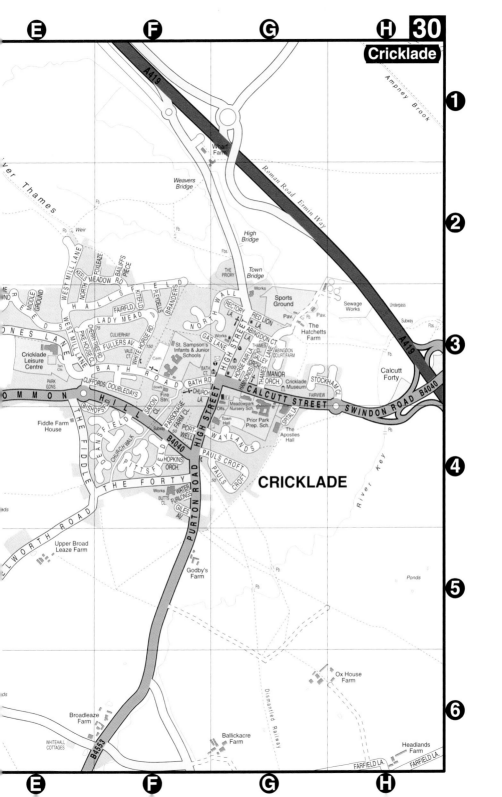

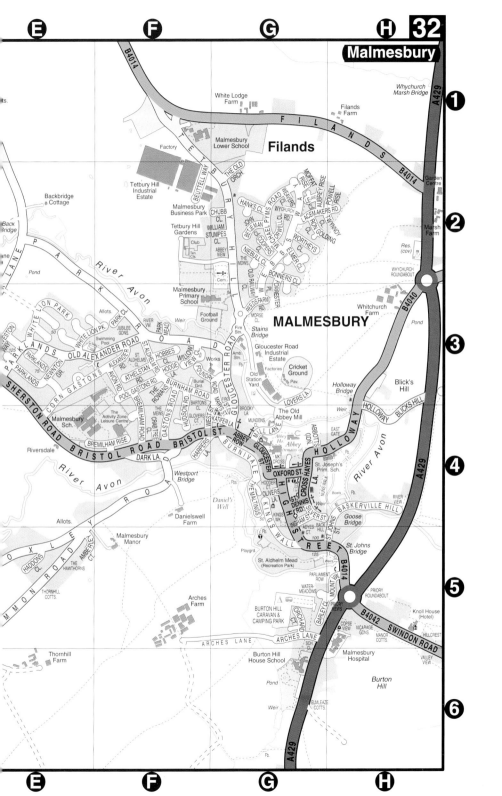

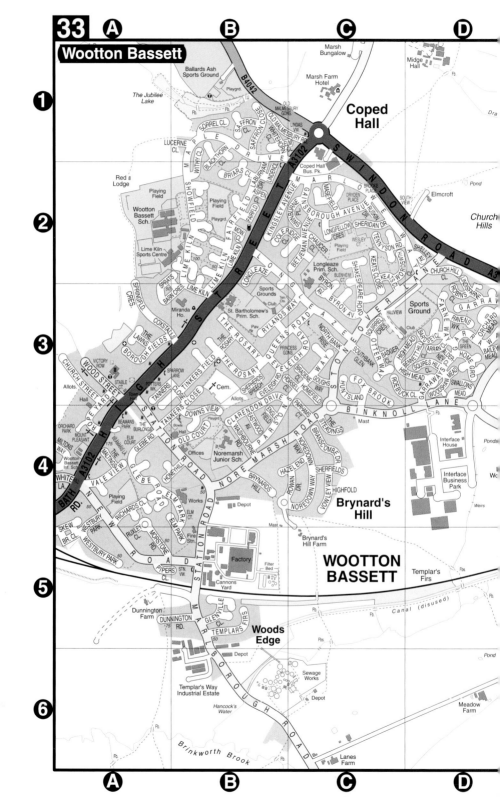

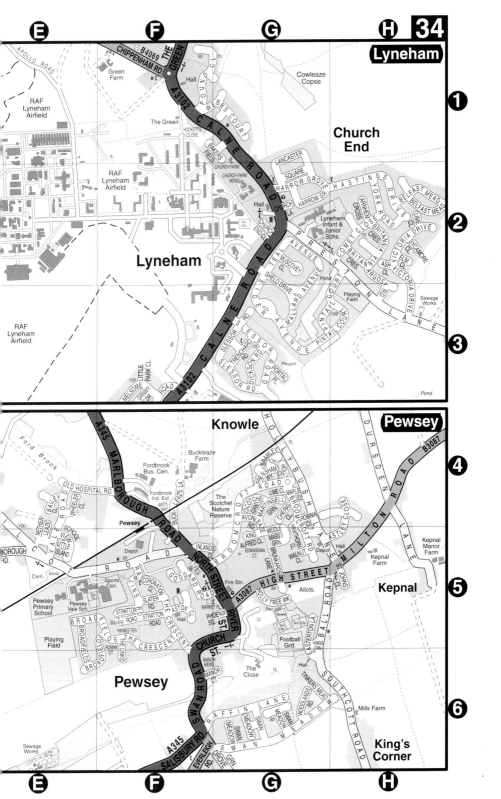

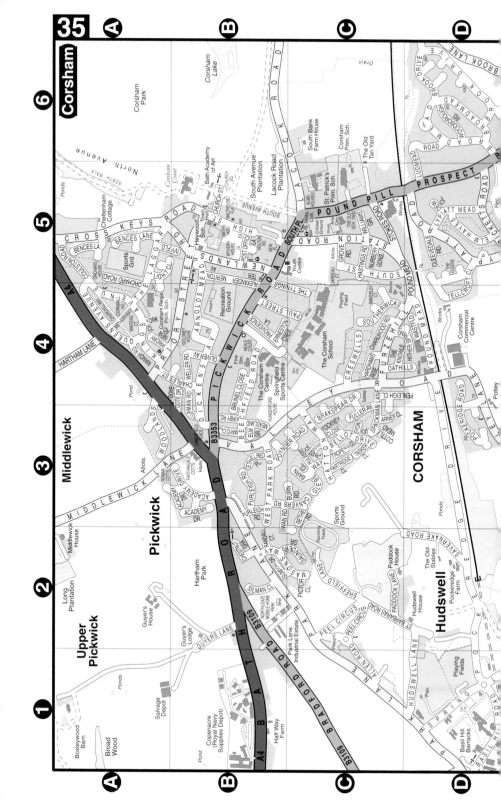

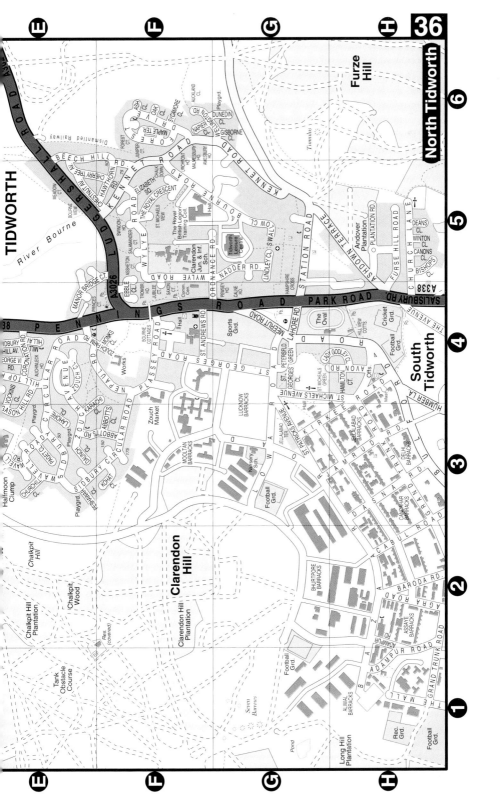

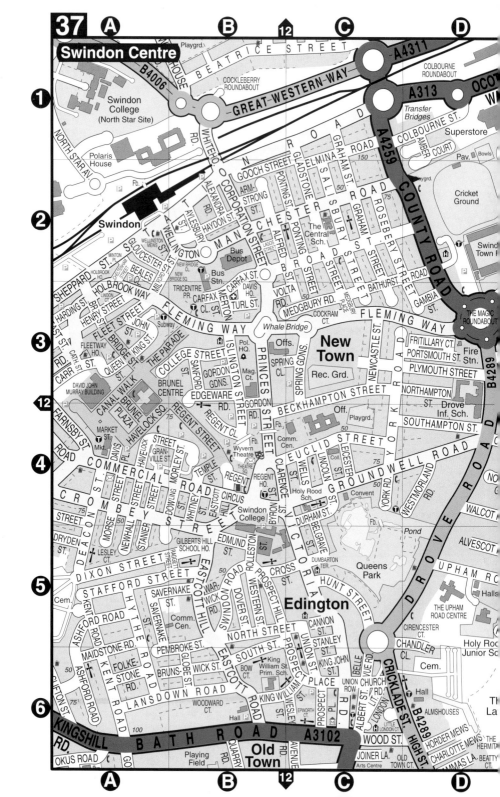

INDEX Abbreviations used

Allot.	Allotment	Coll.	College
Amb.	Ambulance	Comm.	Community
App.	Approach	Comp.	Comprehensive
Arc.	Arcade	Cov.	Covered
Av.	Avenue	Crn.	Corner
Br.	Bridge	Cott(s).	Cottage(s)
Brd.	Broad	Cres.	Crescent
Bldgs.	Buildings	Cft.	Croft
Bung(s).	Bungalow(s)	Ct.	Court
Bus.	Business	Dis.	Disused
Cara.	Caravan	Dr.	Drive
Cem.	Cemetery	E.	East
Cen.	Centre	Ent.	Enterprise
Cl.	Close	Est.	Estate

Fld(s).	Field(s)	Inf.	Infant
Flts.	Flats	Junc.	Junction
Fb.	Footbridge	Jun.	Junior
Gdns.	Gardens	La.	Lane
Gt.	Great	Lib.	Library
Gra.	Grange	Lit.	Little
Grn.	Green	Lwr.	Lower
Grd.	Ground	Mag.	Magistrates
Gr.	Grove	Mdw(s).	Meadow(s)
Hd.	Head	Mem.	Memorial
Hts.	Heights	Mon.	Monument
Ho.	House	Mt.	Mount
Ind.	Industrial	N.	North

Off(s).	Office(s)	S.	South
Orch(s).	Orchard(s)	Sq.	Square
Par.	Parade	Stn.	Station
Pk.	Park	St.	Street
Pass.	Passage	Ten.	Tennis
Pav.	Pavilion	Ter.	Terrace
Pl.	Place	Up.	Upper
Prim.	Primary	Vic.	Vicarage
Rec.	Recreation	Vw.	View
Res.	Reservoir	Vlls.	Villas
Resid.	Residential	Wk.	Walk
Rd.	Road	Wy.	Way
Sch.	School	W.	West
		Yd.	Yard

Use of this Index: An alphabetical order is followed.

1. Each street name is followed by a map reference giving a page number and coordinates: Abberd Lane 29 D3.
2. Names not appearing on the map are shown with an * and the reference of the nearest adjoining street: Back Hill*, Silver Street 32 G4.
3. Where a street name appears more than once the reference is given: Calne Road 34 F1/F2.
4. House numbers along streets are shown as: 250.

A

Abberd Lane................29 D3
Abberd Way................29 C3
Abbey Close................24 H2
Abbey Farm Cottages 1 A5
Abbey Row.................32 G4
Abbey View................32 G2
Abbey View Road..........5 C4
Abbotsbury Way............1 C6
Abbotts Close..............36 F3
Abbotts Garden 32 G4
Abbotts Road..............36 F3
Abingdon Court Farm....30 G3
Abingdon Lane............30 G3
Abington Way..............6 H2
Abney Moor 20 G1
Acacia Close 21 B4
Acacia Grove 6 G4
Academy Drive 35 B3
Acorn Close 14 E4
Adampur Road 36 H1/H2
Addington Close 26 F5
Addison Crescent 7 B4
Aden Court 5 D1
Adwalton Close 10 H5
Adyes Court 32 G5
Affleck Close 11 A4
Agra Road 36 H2
Aiken Road.................5 A2
Ailesbury Close 24 H3
Ailesbury Court*, High Street
...................27 D4
Ainsworth Road 13 C5
Aintree Drive.............23 A1
Akenfield Close 5 D2
Akers Court 2 E3
Akers Way 5 B4/D5
Alan Cobham Road 26 G5
Alanbrooke Crescent 6 E5
Alba Close 10 F1
Albert Street..............37 C6
Albert Terrace*, Bridewell St.
..................26 E4
Albion Place 26 E4
Albion Street............12 E4
Aldborough Close.......11 A2
Aldbourne Close 6 G1
Alder Close.................5 B3
Alderney Close (Wootton B.)
.............15 A1/33 D3
Alexander House*, High St.
...................35 B5
Alexander House*,
Sidbury Circ. Rd. ..36 E4
Alexander Road 32 F3
Alexander Terrace 35 B5
Alexandra Road 37 B2
Alexandra Terrace*,
Blowhorn Street 28 E4

Alfred Bown Court 11 D2
Alfred Street 37 B2
Aliwal Barracks............36 H1
Allen Road 35 C1
Allington Road 6 F2
Allington Way 21 B4
Allison Court 6 E5
Alma Place 27 D4
Alma Terrace 29 B3
Almshouses (Chippenham)
...................21 D6
Almshouses (Swindon) 37 D6
Almshouses*, St. Johns St.
...................32 H5
Almshouses, The (Corsham)
...................35 C5
Alnwick 10 H5
Alpine Close...............10 G2
Alton Close 6 G2
Alvescot Road 37 D5
Alveston Close 11 B3
Amber Court 27 D1
Amberley Close (Calne) 29 A2
Amberley Close (Swindon)
...................6 G3
Amberley Court 32 E5
Ambrose Road 18 G1
Amersham Road 13 D6
Amesbury Close...........6 G1
Amesbury House 36 F5
Anchor Road 29 C4
Ancona Close.............10 G2
Anderson Close 14 F5
Andover Street 12 E4
Andrews Close 21 C6
Angel Yard 27 D4
Angelica Close 5 B3
Angell Close*, Forman Street
...................29 C4
Angler Road 10 H2
Anglesey Close 11 A3
Anglesey Mead 24 H3
Angus Close...............10 H2
Anise Close 5 A3
Anstey Place 24 H3
Anstie Close 26 G3
Ansty Walk 6 F2
Anthony Road.............18 E4
Apollo Road 34 E1
Apple Walk 7 A5
Applewood Close 21 C5
Applewood Court 11 B4
Archer Close..............7 B2
Archers, The 31 B3
Arches Lane 32 F5/G5
Argosy Road 34 H2
Argyle Drive 21 C2
Argyle Street 6 H6
Ark, The 25 D4

Arkwright Road 6 G1
Arley Close 6 E2
Arlington Close.........13 D2
Arliss Close*, Garson Road
.......................6 F1
Armstrong Street 37 B2
Arney Close 35 C3
Arnfield Moor 20 G1
Arnhem Cross 34 H2
Arnolds Mead 35 B4
Arran Close 33 D3
Arran Way 31 B2
Arthur Bennett Court ...12 E4
Arthur Miles Court 7 B3
Artis Avenue 18 F4
Arun Road 25 C5
Arundel Close (Chippenham)
...................21 B6
Arundel Close (Swindon)
...................13 B6
Ascham Road 10 G4
Ascot Close 23 B2
Ash Close (Lyneham)...34 H2
Ash Close (N. Tidworth) 36 F6
Ash Close (Swindon) 4 G5
Ash Gardens 8 G3
Ash Grove 6 G5
Ash Tree Close
(Marlborough) 28 H3
Ash Tree Close (Swindon)
.......................7 C3
Ash Walk 26 H1
Ashburnham Close 10 G5
Ashbury Avenue..........13 D2
Ashcroft Cottages........28 H1
Ashdown Terrace 36 H5
Ashdown Way 5 A3
Ashe Crescent 22 E5
Ashen Copse Road 17 D4
Ashfield Road............22 E4
Ashford Road..........37A5/A6
Ashie Close 4 H5
Ashington Way 11 A4
Ashkirk Close 13 A3
Ashlar Court 12 H6
Ashley Close.............13 B3
Ashmore Close..........14 E3
Ashwell Close............13 B4
Ashworth Road..........11 C3
Askerton Close..........10 F1
Askew Close..............10 F4
Aspen Close.............33 B2
Assaye Barracks 36 H2
Assheton Court........36 F5
Assize Court*, Northgate St.
...................25 D3
Astley Close 34 H5
Aston Bungalows*, Slater Rd.
...................34 F5

Aston Close 34 F5
Aston House*, Slater Road
...................34 F5
Atbara Close..............6 E4
Athelstan Road 32 F3
Athena Avenue...........6 H6
Attlee Crescent 7 B4
Atworth Close 6 F1
Aubrey Close 27 A5
Aubrey Rise 32 G2
Auchinleck House.......36 E4
Auden Close 5 D2
Audley Close 10 F5
Audley Road...............21 D6
Augusta Close............5 A1
Austen Crescent........14 F5
Avebury Close 29 A4
Avebury House*, Welton Rd.
.... 11 B3
Avebury Road (Chippenham)
...................23 B1
Avebury Road (Swindon) 6 F2
Avenel Court 11 D2
Avening Street 6 H6
Avens Close 5 B3
Avenue La Fleche
............22 E6/24 E1
Avenue Road 37 C6
Avenue, The..............36 H4
Avocet Close 14 G3
Avon Close 29 A2
Avon House 12 E6
Avon Mead...............22 G5
Avon Place*, River Street
...................13 C6
Avon Road (Devizes) ...25 A4
Avon Road (Malmesbury)
...................32 F3
Avon Road (N. Tidworth)
...................36 H4
Avon Terrace 25 D3
Avon View*, Bath Rd...25 A4
Avonleaze Road.........34 G4
Avonmead 5 C3/D3
Awdry Close 21 A6
Axbridge Close..........13 C4
Aylesbury Street.........37 B2
Aymer Place 14 E4
Ayr Close 23 A2
Ayrshire Close...........10 H2
Azalea Close............29 C6
Azelin Court 7 D4

B

Babington Park 10 F4
Back Hill...................32 G4
Back Lane (Blunsdon) ...1 D2
Back Lane (Marlborough)
...................27 D4
Back Road 29 B5

Badger Close (Wootton B.)
.......................33 C3
Badgers Close (Devizes)
.......................26 E5
Bagbury Lane 3 A5
Bagbury Park 3 B6
Bailey Close (Devizes) ..26 H1
Bailey Close (Pewsey) ..34 E4
Baileys Corner 11 D1
Baileys Farm Gardens*,
Buckhurst Cres. ..13 C3
Baileys Mead (Swindon) 15 A1
Baileys Mead (Wootton B.)
.......................33 D3
Baileys Way 18 F4
Bailiffs Piece...........30 F2
Bainbridge Close 10 G4
Baird Close................10 H1
Bakehouse Close 22 F6
Bakers Court 7 D5
Bakers Field 34 F1
Bakers Road............18 F6
Bakery Close*, The Street
.......................9 D1
Bakery Mews 7 A3
Balance Row*,
Southbroom Rd....26 E4
Baldwin Close 19 A6
Bale Close 10 F4
Ball Road 34 G5
Balmoral Close (Chippenham)
.......................21 A6
Balmoral Close (Swindon)
.......................13 C6
Bamford Close 3 C2
Bampton Grove 37 D4
Banbury Close 13 A6
Bancroft Close 10 F3
Bank Row*, Church Street
.......................29 B4
Bankfoot Close.........10 H2
Bankside 11 D5
Banwell Avenue 13 C4
Barbury Close 5 D4
Barbury House*, Welton Rd.
.......................11 B3
Barcelona Crescent ...18 E4
Barcote Close...........5 B1
Bardsey Close 33 D3
Barken Road 21 B4
Barkstead Close.......10 H5
Barley Close.............32 G5
Barlow Close 1 C5
Barn Close (Chippenham)
.......................21 B5
Barn Lane (Corsham) ..35 C3
Barn Owl Road.........21 C3
Barn Street 28 E4
Barnard Close 13 D2

Barnfield ... 28 G5
Barnfield Close ... 11 D2
Barnfield Road ... 11 C2
Barnmoor Close ... 14 G6
Barnstaple Close ... 13 D4
Barnum Court ... 12 E2
Baroda Road ... 36 H2
Baron Close ... 7 D4
Barons Mead ... 21 B5
Barra Close ... 31 A3
Barrett Way ... 18 F5
Barrington Close ... 14 F6
Barrow Close ... 28 F4
Barrow Green ... 22 F3
Barrowby Gate ... 7 C3
Barry Glen Close ... 7 A6
Bartholomew House*,
Newlands Road ... 35 B5
Barton Dene ... 27 C4
Barton Road ... 5 C4
Barton, The*, Hudson Road
... 32 F4
Barton, The*, Wood Street
... 33 A3
Bartons Close ... 32 F3
Basil Close ... 5 B3
Basil Hill Barracks ... 35 D1
Basil Hill Road ... 35 D1
Basingstoke Close ... 10 G5
Baskerville Hill ... 32 H4
Baskerville Road ... 14 G2
Bath Court ... 30 F3
Bath Road (Chippenham)
... 22 E6/23 B2
Bath Road (Corsham) ... 35 B1
Bath Road (Cricklade) ... 30 F3
Bath Road (Devizes) ... 25 A4
Bath Road (Marlborough)
... 27 A5
Bath Road (Swindon) ... 37 A6
Bath Road (Wootton B.) 33 A4
Bathampton Street ... 12 E3
Bathurst Road ... 37 C3
Battens, The ... 21 B4
Battlewell ... 3 A4
Baxter Close ... 1 C6
Bay Tree Court ... 6 F5
Baydon Close ... 5 D4
Baydon Grove ... 29 B2
Baydons Lane ... 24 F1
Bayleaf Avenue ... 5 B3
Baylie Acre*, North View Pl.
... 27 D3
Bayliffes Close ... 22 G6
Baywater ... 28 E3
Bazaar Road ... 36 H1
Beach Terrace*, Church St.
... 29 B4
Beacon Close ... 11 D5
Beale Close*, Derriads Lane
... 21 B6
Beales Close ... 37 A2
Beamans Lane ... 33 A4
Beamans Park ... 33 A4
Beatrice Street ... 37 B1
Beatty Court ... 37 D6
Beauchamp Close ... 5 C4
Beauclerc Street ... 25 B4
Beaufort Green ... 13 D4
Beaufort Place ... 18 E6
Beaufort Road ... 18 E4
Beaulieu Close ... 11 A5
Beaumaris Road ... 10 H4
Beaumont Road ... 13 A3
Beaven Close ... 24 G3
Beaversbrook Lane ... 29 A2
Beckhampton Street ... 37 B4
Beddington Court ... 7 C2
Bedford Road ... 13 A3
Bedwyn Close ... 6 G4
Beech Avenue ... 6 E5
Beech Drive ... 4 G5
Beech Grove ... 31 B4
Beech Hill Road ... 36 E6
Beech House Flats*,
Downlands Road ... 26 E6
Beech Lea ... 2 E4
Beechcroft Road ... 6 H4/7 A3
Beeches, The ... 3 B6
Beechfield Drive ... 26 H2
Beechfield Road ... 35 B3
Beechwood Close ... 26 H1
Beechwood Road ... 21 C5
Beehive Close ... 10 G1
Belfast Mead ... 34 H2
Belgrave Street ... 37 C4
Bell Close ... 27 D4
Bell Gardens ... 8 G3
Belle Vue Road (Swindon)
... 37 C6
Bellevue Road (Devizes)
... 25 C3
Bellinger Close ... 21 D2
Bellot Drive ... 35 C3
Bellver ... 10 H4
Belmont Close ... 7 C4
Belmont Crescent ... 12 F6
Belsay ... 11 A5
Belvedere Road ... 13 C6
Bembridge Close ... 13 D5
Bences Lane ... 35 A5
Bennett Hill Close ... 33 C3
Benson Close ... 27 B5
Bentham Close ... 11 B3
Bentley Close ... 13 C3
Bentley Grove ... 29 C4
Bentley Lane ... 29 C6
Benwell Close ... 11 A3
Berenger Close ... 12 H6
Beresford Close ... 14 E5
Bergamot Close ... 27 A5
Bergman Close ... 6 F1
Berkeley Close ... 21 B6
Berkeley Lawns ... 13 B6
Berkeley Road ... 18 F4
Berkshire Drive ... 10 G2
Berkshire House ... 13 B1
Berricot Lane ... 20 G5
Berrington Road ... 13 C6
Berry Copse ... 4 F6
Berrycroft ... 28 H3
Berton Close ... 2 E3
Berwick Way ... 6 G3
Bess Road ... 10 F5
Bessemer Close ... 6 E6
Bessemer Road East ... 6 E6
Bessemer Road West ... 5 D6
Bethany House ... 6 G6
Bethel Road ... 35 C2
Betjeman Avenue ... 33 C2
Betjeman Road ... 27 A5
Betony Close ... 5 C2
Beuttell Way ... 32 F2
Bevan Close ... 7 B4
Beverley ... 11 A5
Beverley Way ... 23 A2
Beverstone Grove ... 13 B5
Bevil ... 10 G6
Bevisland ... 14 E6
Bhurtpore Barracks ... 36 G2
Bibury Road ... 13 A4
Bicton Road ... 5 D1
Biddel Springs ... 31 D3
Bideford Close ... 13 C4
Bilborough Drive ... 13 B4
Bill Turpin Court ... 13 D5
Bindon Close ... 10 F4
Binknoll Lane ... 33 C4
Birch Grove ... 22 F4
Birch Street ... 11 D4
Birches, The ... 19 C1
Birchwood Road ... 7 D5
Birdbrook Road ... 7 A2
Birdcombe Road ... 11 A4
Birds Marsh View ... 22 E3
Bishop Close (Chippenham)
... 24 G3
Bishop Road ... 29 B3
Bishopdale Close ... 4 G6
Bishops Close (N. Tidworth)
... 36 H5
Bishopsfield ... 30 E4
Bisley Close ... 13 C4
Bittern Road ... 14 G3
Blackberry Close ... 21 B3
Blackbridge Road ... 22 G5
Blackcross ... 24 G1
Blacklands ... 3 A3
Blackman Gardens*,
Queintin Road ... 12 H6
Blackmore Close ... 14 G2
Blackstone Avenue ... 14 E5
Blackthorn Close ... 33 B2
Blackthorn Lane ... 6 F4
Blackthorn Mews ... 24 G2
Blackwellhams ... 24 F2
Blackworth ... 31 B1
Bladen Close ... 17 D5
Blagrove House ... 12 H5
Blair Parade ... 5 D4
Blake Crescent ... 8 E5
Blakeney Avenue ... 13 D2
Blakesley Close ... 13 B5
Blandford Alley ... 31 C4
Blandford Court ... 13 D3
Blenheim Court ... 33 C2
Blenheim Road ... 18 E4
Bletchley Close ... 14 E5
Blicks Hill ... 32 H4
Blind Lane ... 30 E5
Bloomsbury Close ... 10 G5
Blowhorn Street ... 27 D3
Blowhorn Street ... 28 E3
Bluebell Drive ... 21 C2
Bluebell Grove ... 29 B2
Bluebell Path ... 5 C2
Blunsdon Abbey
Caravan Park ... 1 B5
Blunsdon Hill ... 1 B2
Blunsdon Road ... 5 D2/D3
Bob May Court ... 14 E4
Bodiam Drive ... 11 A6/B4
Bodiam Drive North*,
Bodiam Drive ... 11 B4
Bodiam Drive South*,
Bodam Drive ... 11 B5
Bodman Close ... 24 G3
Bodmin Close ... 13 C3
Boldrewood ... 14 F6
Boleyn Close ... 10 G3
Bolingbroke Close ... 9 A3
Bolingbroke Road ... 5 C5
Bolts Croft ... 24 F1
Boness Road ... 18 E4
Bonner Close ... 10 F4
Bonners Close ... 32 G2
Boothmead ... 21 C5
Borage Close ... 5 B2
Borough Fields ... 33 A3
Borough Parade*, High St.
... 22 F6
Boscombe Road ... 5 C3
Bosham Close ... 10 H5
Bosworth Road ... 10 G4
Botany ... 31 A4
Bothwell Road ... 3 B2
Botley Copse*, Letterage Rd.
... 4 G5
Boulevard, The ... 5 A2
Boundary Close ... 7 A2
Boundary Road ... 22 G5
Bourne Cottages ... 36 F4
Bourne Road (N. Tidworth)
... 36 G5
Bourne Road (Swindon)
... 5 C5/D4
Bourne View ... 36 E5
Bourton Avenue ... 7 D5
Bouverie Avenue ... 13 A6
Bow Court ... 37 B6
Bowes Court*,
Thomas Wyatt Rd. 26 E6
Bowles Road ... 6 E2
Bowleymead ... 14 F3/F4
Bowling Green Lane ... 12 G6
Bowman Close ... 7 D4
Bowood Road ... 12 E5
Boydell Close ... 10 H1
Bradbury Close ... 24 H2
Bradene Close ... 33 C3
Bradenham Road ... 10 G4
Bradford Road (Corsham)
... 35 C1
Bradford Road (Swindon)
... 12 G5
Bradley Road ... 6 H3
Bradwell Moor ... 20 F1
Braemar Close ... 13 B6
Braemor Road ... 29 A3
Brain Court ... 7 C5
Brake Mead ... 22 G6
Brakspear Drive ... 35 C3
Bramble Close ... 7 A6
Bramble Drive ... 24 G3
Bramble Road ... 7 A5/A6/B5
Bramdean Close*,
Elstree Way ... 5 D1
Bramley Close ... 34 G4
Bramptons, The ... 10 H2
Bramwell Close ... 7 A1
Branders ... 30 F3
Brandon Close ... 10 G4
Branksome Road ... 5 C4
Branscombe Drive ... 33 C4
Bratton Avenue ... 26 F5
Bratton Close ... 6 F2
Braybrook Close ... 10 F1
Braydon Court*, Sherston Av.
... 6 G2
Breach, The ... 26 E5
Bream Close ... 29 A2
Brecon Close ... 19 A1
Bremhill Close ... 6 G3
Bremhill View ... 29 A2
Bremilham Rise ... 32 E4
Bremilham Road ... 32 F3
Brendon Walk ... 13 D3
Brettingham Gate ... 19 B3
Brewer Mead ... 24 G2
Brewers Lane ... 29 C5
Brewery Street ... 31 C4
Briarfields ... 13 A1
Briars Close ... 33 B2
Briarswood Court ... 14 F6
Brickham Road ... 26 F3
Brickley ... 26 G4
Brickley Lane ... 26 F3/H6
Bricksteed Avenue ... 26 F4
Bridewell Square ... 26 E4
Bridewell Street ... 26 E4
Bridge End Road ... 7 B6
Bridge Street (Marlborough)
... 27 A5
Bridge Street (Swindon) 37 A3
Bridge, The ... 22 E6
Bridgeman Close ... 7 D5
Bridgemead Close ... 11 B2
Bridgewater Close ... 12 E2
Bridport Road ... 13 D5
Briery Close ... 7 C3
Bright Close ... 24 G2
Bright Street ... 12 H1
Brighton Way ... 23 A1
Brimble Hill ... 18 G6
Brind Close ... 14 G3
Brindley Close ... 5 B6
Brington Road ... 13 D1
Brinkworth Close ... 21 A6
Bristol Road (Chippenham)
... 21 A3/C4
Bristol Street (Swindon) 12 E3
Bristol Street (Malmesbury)
... 32 E4
Britannia Crescent ... 34 H2
Britannia Place ... 12 H5
Brittain Close ... 21 A6
Brittox, The ... 26 E3
Brixham Avenue ... 13 A4
Broad Street ... 37 B2
Broadfields ... 34 E5
Broadleas Close ... 25 D5
Broadleas Crescent ... 25 D5
Broadleas Park ... 25 D5
Broadleas Road ... 25 D5
Broadmead ... 35 D6
Broadmead Walk ... 13 D2
Broadmoor Road ... 8 F1
Broadway ... 6 E4
Brockley Rise ... 7 C2
Broken Cross ... 29 B3
Bromley Close ... 13 A3
Bronte Close ... 14 F5
Brook Drive ... 35 D6
Brook Street ... 21 C5
Brook Way ... 29 C4
Brookdene ... 5 C3
Brookdene Lodge ... 5 C3
Brooke Close ... 10 F1
Brooke Cresent ... 5 A2
Brooke Place ... 33 C2
Brookfield ... 31 B2
Brooklands Avenue ... 5 D6
Brooklime Close ... 5 A3
Brookmeadow Caravan Park
... 18 E6
Brooks Close ... 7 A2
Brooksby Way ... 13 D1
Brookwell Close ... 21 D3
Brooky Lane ... 32 G4
Broomcroft Road ... 34 G5
Broome Manor Lane ... 19 A1
Broomfield ... 22 E3
Brotherton Close ... 24 G2
Broughton Grange ... 13 B5
Brow, The ... 5 C3
Browning Close ... 7 D4
Bruce Street ... 11 D2
Bruddel Grove ... 19 A1
Bruges Close ... 22 G6
Brunel Centre ... 37 A3
Brunel Close ... 35 B3
Brunel Court (Chippenham)
... 23 C1
Brunel Court (Marlborough)
... 28 F4
Brunel Plaza ... 37 A3
Brunkards Lane ... 34 G5
Brunswick Street ... 37 A6
Bruton Walk ... 13 C5
Bryans Close Road ... 29 B3
Bryanston Way ... 14 E3
Bryant Road ... 5 A2
Brynards Hill ... 33 B4
Bryony Way ... 5 B3
Buckhurst Crescent ... 13 C3
Buckingham Road
(Chippenham) ... 24 H2
Buckingham Road (Swindon)
... 13 B6
Buckland Close ... 13 D3
Buckleaze Lane ... 34 F4
Bucklebury Close ... 7 C6
Buckthorn Drive ... 5 B3
Bude Road ... 11 D3
Buie Close ... 4 H5
Bulford Road ... 36 H3
Buller Street ... 6 H6
Bullfinch Close ... 14 F3/G3
Bulls Hill ... 22 F6
Bumpers Way ... 21 A5

Bunce Road 7 C5
Bungalows, The (Swindon) 6 F5
Bungalows, The*, Horton Rd. 26 H1
Bungalows, The*, Abberd Way..........29 C3
Buntings, The 14 F2
Burbage Road 6 G1
Burcot Close*, Cookham Rd. 5 A1
Burden Close 8 E6
Burderop Close..............18 F3
Burford Avenue 13 A4
Burgess Close 7 C6
Burghley Close.............13 B3
Burlands Road 24 F1
Burleaze.......................23 D2
Burlongs, The...............33 A4
Burn Road 35 C3
Burnet Close....................5 B3
Burnham Court..............26 E6
Burnham Road (Malmesbury) 32 F3
Burnham Road (Swindon) 13 D3
Burnivale 32 G4
Burns Way 7 A3
Burton Hill Caravan & Camping Park 32 G5
Bury Fields 3 D6
Burytown Lane 2 E3
Bute Close 31 B2
Buttercup Close 21 C2
Buttermere 14 G6
Butterworth Street 12 E4
Butts Close 30 F4
Butts Road 19 B5
Butts, The (Chippenham) 24 F1
Butts, The (Lydiard Millicent) 9 C1
Bydemill Gardens..........31 A4
Byfield Way 13 D1
Byrd Close 10 F4
Byron Avenue..........33 C2/C3
Byron Court 8 G2
Byron Road 26 E6
Byron Street 37 B4
Bythebrook....................21 C4
C
Cabot Drive....................10 F3
Cabul Road 36 H2
Cadley Close 6 G5
Caen Hill.......................25 A4
Caen Hill Gardens 25 A4
Caernarvon Walk 19 B1
Cagney Drive 6 E1
Caird Lawns 26 F5
Cairndow Way 7 A2
Calcutt Street 30 G3
Calder Close.............5 D2/D3
Callaghan Close.............7 C5
Callenders 11 C4
Callington Road 4 H1
Calne House 36 G4
Calne Road 34 F1/F2
Calstock Road 4 H1
Calvert Road 13 A3
Cambria Bridge Road....12 E4
Cambria Cottages 8 G2
Cambria Court*, Curtis St. 12 F4
Cambria Place 12 E4
Cambridge Close 13 B5
Camdale Parade 6 H6
Camden Close..............10 G4
Cameron Close 7 C6
Campden Road 13 A4
Campfield House*, Thomas Wyatt Rd. 26 E6
Campion Close..............29 B2
Campion Gate 10 F4
Camton Road 10 F2
Canal Close 29 A5
Canal Road...................24 F3
Canal Walk....................37 A4
Canal Way 26 H1
Candahar Barracks 36 H3
Canford Close 14 E3
Canney Close................19 B6
Canney, The..................19 B6
Cannon Street 37 C5
Canons Close................36 H5
Cantelo Close..................1 B6
Canterbury Close 13 B6
Canterbury Street..........21 D5
Capesthorne Drive 5 C1
Capitol Close 8 F6
Caprice Close 10 F2
Caraway Drive 5 A3
Cardigan Close..............13 A5
Cardigan Road..............27 C4
Cardwell Close 13 D2
Carey Close 10 G4
Carfax Close.................37 B3
Carfax Street 37 B3
Carisbrooke Terrace......19 A6
Carlisle Avenue 12 H6
Carlton Gate..................19 B2
Carlton Terrace 25 C3
Carman Close 7 D4
Carnarvon Close 21 B6
Carnegie Mews 29 B4
Carnegie Road.............29 C2
Carp Road 29 A2
Carpenter Close............24 G2
Carpenter Court 12 H1
Carpenters Lane 12 H1
Carr Street 37 A3
Carrick Close 22 H5
Carroll Close..................14 F5
Carronbridge Road........10 H3
Carshalton Road 13 D6
Carstairs Avenue 13 C6
Carter Close...................6 G1
Cartmell Court*, Ingram St. 32 G4
Cartwright Drive 10 G1
Cary Glen......................24 H3
Casson Road 7 C5
Castilian Mews*, Ramleaze Drive....10 G2
Castle Court (Devizes)..25 D4
Castle Court (Marlborough) 27 D5
Castle Dore 10 G4
Castle Grounds*, Castle La. 25 D4
Castle Hill Cottages 2 F2
Castle Lane 25 D4
Castle Road 25 D4
Castle Street.................29 B4
Castle View Close 19 B5
Castle View Road (Chiseldon) 19 B5
Castle View Road (Strat. St. Margaret) 8 E6
Castle Walk 29 A4
Castlefield Close 10 H3
Castlefields...................29 A4
Castlehaven Close........24 H2
Castleton Road..............10 F2
Catherine Street 37 A3
Catherine Wayte Close ..5 D3
Catmint Close.................5 B3
Catterick Close..............23 A2
Caulfield Road 12 H1
Causeway......................22 F6
Causeway Close*, Causeway 22 F6
Cavalier Court 21 A5
Cavendish Square 13 C5
Caversham Close..........13 B4
Cavie Close 10 G1
Caxton Close 13 B5
Caxton Court*, Caxton Close 13 B5
Cayenne Park..................5 A3
Cecil Road 13 C3
Cedar Grove..................22 F4
Cedar House Flats*, Downlands Road ..26 E6
Cedars Close 6 E5
Cedars, The 3 B3
Celandine Way..............21 C3
Centurion Close 24 H2
Centurion Way 14 E1
Century Close 26 G4
Chalford Avenue 13 D2
Chalgrove Field 10 G6
Chalk Down 36 F5
Chamberlain Road (Chippenham) 21 A5
Chamberlain Road (Swindon) 7 C5
Chancellor Close 10 F3
Chandler Close (Devizes) 26 G4
Chandler Close (Swindon) 37 C5
Chandler Way*, Fox Croft Wk. 24 G3
Chandlers Yard 27 D4
Chandos Close 10 G3
Chantry Court................26 E3
Chantry Lane 27 D5
Chantry Road..................5 D5
Chapel Court*, Thomas Wyatt Rd. 26 E6
Chapel Court*, The Elms 31 B4
Chapel Hill 1 D3
Chapel House*, Mead Way 11 A2
Chapel Lane (Swindon) ..8 G3
Chapel Lane (Chippenham) 22 F6
Chapel Lane Cottages 8 G2
Chapel Street 12 H1
Chaplins Terrace*, Luggershall Road..36 E5
Chapter Close 28 G5
Charfield Close 13 C5
Charlbury Close 5 D4
Charles Macpherson Gardens 14 E4
Charles Morrison Close 25 D4
Charles Street 35 B4
Charlieu Avenue*, Stockley Lane 29 D6
Charlock Path*, Windflower Road 5 C2
Charlotte Mews 37 D6
Charlton Close 6 H2
Charlwood Road 35 C4
Charminster Close 14 E3
Charnwood Court..........12 H6
Charolais Drive 10 G2
Charter Close................26 G2
Charter House Road 17 D5
Charter Road 22 E6
Chartley Green.............10 G4
Chase Wood 4 G5
Chatsworth Road 5 D2
Chaucer Close 33 C2
Chaveywell Court..........29 A4
Cheddar Road 5 C4
Chedworth Gate...........19 B2
Chelmsford Road 11 A2
Cheltenham Drive..........23 B2
Cheltenham Street 37 A2
Cheltenham Villas 25 B4
Chelwood Close............23 C1
Chelworth Road 30 E5
Cheney Manor Road 5 D6/6 E4/11 D1
Chepstow Close (Chippenham) 23 B2
Chepstow Close (Swindon)..............11 A6
Chequers, The*, St. Johns St. 25 D4
Cheraton Close 13 D2
Cherbury Walk*, Courtenay Road ..13 C3
Cherhill Court..................5 C4
Cherry Brier Close 9 D1
Cherry Close 34 G4
Cherry Orchard (Highworth) 31 C3
Cherry Orchard (Malmesbury) 28 E5
Cherry Tree Avenue 36 F5
Cherry Tree Court 29 B2
Cherry Tree Grove..........6 G5
Cherry Tree Road..........30 E3
Chervil Close 5 A3
Chesford Road..............13 C6
Chester Street 12 F3
Chester Way.................23 B2
Chesterfield Close*, Silchester Way......11 A3
Chesters, The...............11 A3
Chestnut Avenue (N. Tidworth) 36 F5
Chestnut Avenue (Swindon) 6 G4
Chestnut Drive 28 D5
Chestnut Grange 35 B2
Chestnut Road 21 D5
Chestnut Springs 9 D1
Chevalier Close 10 F2
Cheviot Close................10 G3
Chevral Close................21 C3
Chickerell Road 13 C3/C4
Chicory Close 5 A4
Chilton Gardens 5 D4
Chilworth Close 5 C2
Chiminage Close 27 D3
Chippenham Road 34 F1
Chippenham Walk*, Hannington Close ..6 F1
Chiseldon Court 19 A6
Chiseldon House*, Welton Road 11 B3
Chissell Brook*, Bishop Stokes Cft. 29 B3
Chivers Road (Devizes) 26 G4
Chivers Road*, Rowe Mead 24 F2
Chives Way 5 B3
Chobham Close 7 C2
Chopping Knife Lane 28 G5
Christie Close 14 F5
Christopher Drive 24 H3
Chubb Close..................32 F2
Chudleigh......................10 H5
Church Hill Close (Wootton B.) 33 D2
Church Buildings 8 H3
Church End Close 34 G2
Church Farm 34 G2
Church Farm Cottages..28 H3
Church Farm Lane 8 H3
Church Farm Mews 34 G2
Church Ground................8 H3
Church Hill 17 D6
Church Lane (Cricklade) 30 F3
Church Lane (Lyneham) 34 G2
Church Lane (Marlborough) 28 H3
Church Lane (N. Tidworth) 36 H5
Church Path 3 C4
Church Place (Lydiard Millicent) ..3 C6
Church Place (Swindon)12 E3
Church Road (Malmesbury) 32 G2
Church Road (Swindon)37 C6
Church Square 35 B5
Church Street (Calne) ..29 B4
Church Street (Chiseldon) 19 A5
Church Street (Corsham) 35 B5
Church Street (Pewsey) 34 F5
Church Street (Purton)....3 C3
Church Street (Strat. St. Margaret) 7 D4
Church Street (Wootton B.) 33 A3
Church View (Chippenham) 21 D3
Church View (Highworth) 31 B3
Church Walk (Cricklade) 30 F4
Church Walk (Devizes)..26 F4
Church Walk (Swindon) ..7 A4
Church Walk North..........5 D4
Church Walk South 5 D4
Church Way (Blunsden) ..2 E3
Church Way (Strat. St. Margaret) 7 D5
Churchfield......................5 D3
Churchill Avenue 2 E3
Churchill Close (Calne) 29 C5
Churchill Close (Hook) 9 A6
Churchill Close (N. Tidworth) 36 E3
Churchill Court 28 E4
Churchill Way 35 A4
Churchward Avenue........6 E6
Churchward Court 22 E5
Cinders End*, Lowden Av. 22 E5
Circle, The 6 G4
Cirencester Court..........37 D5
Cirencester Way 6 H5/H6/12 H1
Clanfield Road 13 D4
Clardon Lane 3 C1
Clare Walk 10 H5
Claremont Court..............6 F4
Claremont Villas*, Bath Road 25 B4
Clarence Road 21 A6
Clarence Street 37 B4
Clarendon Cottages 12 E4
Clarendon Court*, Wylye Rd. 36 F5
Clarendon Drive 33 B4
Clark Avenue 29 C2
Clarke Drive 10 H1
Clary Road 5 A3
Clayhill Copse 4 G5
Claypole Mead 24 F2
Clays Close 7 A4
Cleasby Close 11 B3
Cleeve Lawns................13 B6
Cleeve, The 35 D5
Cleevedale Road 35 D5
Cleeves Close 10 G3
Clevedon Close 13 C3
Cleverton Court 6 G2
Cliffords 30 E3
Clift Avenue 22 F4
Clift House 22 E5
Clifton Close.................21 C5
Clifton Street.................37 A6
Clinton Close 10 F5
Clive Parade....................6 H4
Cloche Way 7 A4
Clock Tower Lodge*, Thomas Wyatt Rd. 26 E6

Cloisters, The*, Gipsy Lane 24 E1
Close, The (Chippenham) 24 G1
Close, The (Lydiard Millicent) 9 D1
Cloudberry Road 5 C2
Clover Dean 23 B1
Clover Park 5 B3
Cloverlands 5 B3
Club Buildings*, Park Lane 22 E5
Clyde Cottages 18 F3
Clydesdale Close 10 G2
Coatside Way 20 F2
Cobbett Close 1 C6
Cobden Road 12 E1
Cocklebury Close 22 G5
Cocklebury Cottages 22 G5
Cocklebury Lane 22 F3
Cocklebury Road 22 F5
Cockram Court 37 C3
Coffin Close*, Westrop ..31 B3
Colbert Park 5 D1
Colbourne Close 24 H2
Colbourne Street 37 C1
Colchester Close 11 B5
Coldharbour Lane 28 E3
Cole Close 14 F3
Colebrook Close 7 D6
Colebrook Road 13 D1
Colemans Close 29 C4
Coleridge Close 33 B2
Coleridge Road 5 D1
College Close 22 G5
College Court*, Eastcott Hill 37 B4
College Fields 27 B5
College Road 3 C3
College Street 37 A3
Collen Close 21 A6
Collett Avenue 6 E6
Collingsmead 14 E4
Collins Court 36 E3
Collins Lane 3 C3
Coln Crescent 6 E3
Colston Close 13 C5
Colston Road 25 D3
Comet Close 34 H2
Comfrey Close 5 B3
Commercial Road (Devizes) 25 D3
Commercial Road (Swindon) 37 A4
Common Hill 30 E3
Common Road 32 E5
Common Slip 22 F6
Common, The (Marlborough) 27 D3
Common, The (Purton) 3 B1
Commonweal Road 12 F6
Compton Close 14 E5
Conan Doyle Walk 14 F5
Conisborough 11 A4
Coniston Road 23 A1
Connelly Close 5 A2
Conrad Close 14 F5
Consciences Lane 25 A1
Constable Road 7 A5
Constantine Close 8 E1
Conway Road (Chippenham) 21 B6
Conway Road (Swindon) 14 E6
Conyers Close 10 F5
Cooke Court*, Thomas Wyatt Rd. 26 E6
Cookham Road 5 A1
Coombe Close 18 G6
Coombe Road 5 D4
Cooper Fields 6 E2
Coopers Close 32 G2
Cop Close 29 B4
Copes Yard 28 E4
Copings Close 26 E4
Copper Beeches 31 B4
Coppice Close 5 B4
Copse Avenue 13 A1
Copse View 32 H5
Copse, The*, Chapel Hill ..1 D3
Corby Avenue 13 A6
Corfe Close 6 E3
Corfe Crescent 29 A3
Corfe Road 10 H5
Coriander Way 5 B2
Corinium Way 14 E1
Corn Gastons 32 E4
Cornerfields 28 F4
Cornfield Road 26 G4
Cornflower Close 29 C2
Cornflower Road 5 B2
Cornmarsh Way 14 G2
Cornwall Avenue 6 E6
Cornwall Crescent 25 D5
Cornwall House 35 A4
Coronation Close 34 F5
Coronation Road (N. Tidworth) 36 E4
Coronation Road (Wroughton) 18 E5
Coronation Villas*, Salisbury Street 25 B4
Corporation Street 37 B2
Corral Close 4 G6
Corsham Road 6 G2
Corton Crescent 10 H3
Costow 16 H3
Cote Close 10 H1
Cotswold Close 29 D4
Cotswold Way 31 B3
Cottages, The*, Snuff Street 25 D3
Cottars Close 7 D4
Cottington Close 10 G5
Cottle Mead 35 C3
Couch Lane 25 D3
Coulston Road 35 A5
County Road 37 D2
Courtenay Road 13 C3
Courtsknap Court 12 E4
Coventry Close 18 F4
Covingham Drive 14 E2/F1
Covingham Square 14 E2
Cowbridge Crescent*, Swindon Road 32 H5
Cowdrey Close 10 H5
Cowleaze Crescent 17 D5
Cowleaze Walk 7 A3
Cowley Walk 13 D4
Cowslip Close 26 G2
Cowslip Grove 29 B2
Cowslip Way 21 C2
Coxs Hill 29 B4
Coxstalls 33 A3
Crab Tree Close 32 F4
Crabbes Close 27 C4
Crabtree Copse 4 G5
Crammer Court*, Church Wk. 26 F4
Crampton Road 13 C2
Cranborne Chase 5 A3
Crane Furlong 31 C2
Cranesbill Close 26 G2
Cranmore Avenue 13 C5
Cranwell Close 23 B1
Crawford Close 10 G5
Crawley Avenue 7 D5
Crescent, The (Chiseldon) 19 A6
Crescent, The (Pewsey) 34 F5
Crescent, The (Swindon) 4 G5
Creswells 35 C4
Cricketts Lane 24 G2
Cricklade Court*, Cricklade Street 37 C6
Cricklade Road (Highworth) 31 A4
Cricklade Road (Puton) ..2 E6
Cricklade Road (Swindon) 2 E6/6 G1/H6
Cricklade Street 37 C6
Crieff Close 13 D3
Crispin Close 7 D4
Croft Court 23 B2
Croft Road 12 G6/18 F2/G3
Croft, The*, Arches La. 32 G5
Crombey Street 37 A4
Cromer Court*, Liden Drive 14 F6
Crompton Road 6 H1
Cromwell 10 H6
Cromwell Court 27 D5
Cromwell Road 26 G5
Crosby Walk 13 C6
Cross Hayes Lane 32 G4
Cross Hayes*, Cross Hayes La. ..32 G4
Cross Keys Road 35 A5
Cross Lane 27 D4
Cross Patch 27 D4
Cross Roads*, London Road 26 H1
Cross Street 37 B5
Crossing Lane 22 H2
Crossways Avenue 6 G4
Crosswood Road 13 C5
Crouch Farm Cottages*, Lechlade Road 31 C3
Crown Close 24 H2
Crown Court*, Gordon Gdns. 37 B3
Crudwell Way 6 G1
Cruse Close 21 A5
Cuckoos Mead 14 G3
Cullerne Road 8 E6
Cullerns, The 31 C3
Culverhay 30 F3
Culvermead Close 28 E4
Culverwell Road 21 B6
Culvery Court*, Harding St. 12 F3
Cumberland Road 37 D4
Cunetio Road 14 E1
Cunningham House*, Sidbury Circ. Rd. ..36 E4
Cunningham Road 6 E5
Cunnington Close 26 G3
Curlew Drive 21 B3
Curnicks, The 19 A6
Curtis Street 12 F4
Curzon Close 29 A4
Curzon Street 29 A4
Cygnet Close 26 H1
Cyppa Court 24 F1
Cypress Grove 6 E4
Cyprus Terrace*, Northgate Street ..25 D3
D
Dacre Road 13 C3
Daisy Close 5 A4
Dalefoot Close 4 F6
Dales Close 1 C6
Dallas Avenue 13 D2
Dallas Road 21 D5
Dalton Close 13 B2
Dalwood Close 13 D6
Dammas Lane 12 H5
Dando Drive 27 B5
Danes Close 24 G2
Danestone Close 10 F2
Daniel Close 11 D5
Daniel Gooch House 11 D2
Daniell Drive 24 F1
Daniels Court 19 B5
Danvers Mead 24 H3
Danvers Road 35 C3
Darby Close 5 C6
Darcey Close (Swindon) 10 F3
Darcy Close (Chippenham) 22 G5
Darius Way 6 E1
Dark Lane 32 F4
Darnley Close 13 B3
Dart Avenue 6 E4
Dartmoor Close 11 D5
Darwin Close 13 D2
Dasna Road 36 H3
Daunch Close 36 E3
Dauntsey House*, Welton Rd. 11 B3
Dave Watkins Court 7 B4
Davenham Close 13 C6
Davenwood 7 B3
David John Murray Building 37 A3
David Stoddart Gardens ..6 F6
Davies Close 27 A5
Davies Drive 26 H1
Davis House 37 B3
Davis Place 37 A4
Dawlish Road 13 D4
Day House Lane 20 E1
Days Close 7 C6
Deacon Street 37 A5
Deacons Court 1 D3
Dean Street 11 D4
Deans Close 36 H5
Deansfield 30 F4
Deansway 22 E3
Deansway Court 22 E3
Deben Crescent 5 D2
Deburgh Street 11 D3
Deerhurst Way 11 B5
Delamere Drive 7 C3
Delhi Barracks 36 H3
Denbeck Wood 10 H2
Denbigh Close 13 A6
Denholme Road 13 C6
Denton Court 7 D5
Derby Close 24 G2
Derby Court 13 A3
Derriads Court 23 A1
Derriads Green 21 B6
Derriads Lane 21 A6
Derwent Drive 7 B3
Desborough 10 G6
Deva Close 14 F1
Devereux Close 10 F4
Devizes House*, Wylye Rd. 36 F5
Devizes Road (Devizes) 25 A1
Devizes Road (Swindon) 12 H6
Devizes Road (Wroughton) 18 F5
Devon Close 23 A1
Devon Road 6 E6
Dew Close 35 D5
Dewberry Close 5 C3
Dewell Mews 12 H6
Dewey Close 19 B5
Deweys Place*, North Street 34 F5
Dexter Close 10 H2
Dianmer Close 9 A4
Dickens Avenue 35 B3
Dickens Close 14 F5/F6
Dickenson Road 5 A2
Dicketts Road 35 D5
Dickson Road 34 G3
Dickson Way 24 G2
Dinmore Road 5 D1
Dixon Street 37 A5
Dixon Way 29 B3
Dobbin Close 14 G2
Dobson Close 1 C5
Dockle Way 7 B3
Doctor Behr Court*, The Bungalows 6 F5
Dogridge 3 A4
Don Close 6 E3
Doncaster Close*, Beverley Way 23 A2
Donnington Grove 13 B5
Dorcan Way 13 C1/D6/14 E2/E6
Dorchester Road 13 B6
Dores Court 6 H4
Doris Archer Court 6 F5
Dormers, The 31 C2/C3
Dorset Green 5 D5
Doubledays 30 F3
Douglas Road 13 B3
Dovecote Drive 35 B4
Dover Street (Chippenham) 21 D6
Dover Street (Swindon) 37 B5
Dovetrees 14 F2
Dowlais Close 5 A1
Dowling Street 37 A4
Down View (Chippenham) 21 B6
Downham Mead 22 G5
Downing Street 21 D5
Downland Road (Calne) 29 A4
Downland Road (Swindon) 5 B3
Downs Road 19 B5
Downs View (Highworth) 31 C3
Downs View (Wootton B.) 33 B4
Downs View Road 19 B1
Downs Way 20 G2
Downs, The 26 G4
Downslands Road 26 E6
Downton Road 6 F2
Doyle Close 5 A2
Drake Cresent 23 A1
Drakes Avenue 26 F5
Drakes Way 13 B2
Drakes Way Close 13 A3
Draycott Close 13 C4
Draycott Road 19 A6
Drayton Walk 13 B3
Drew Street 11 C2
Drews Pond Lane 26 E6
Drive, The 13 D3/14 E3
Drove Road 37 D5
Druids Close 29 A4
Drury Close 9 A3
Dryden Place 33 C2
Dryden Street 37 A5
Duchess Way 7 A2
Ducks Meadow 27 D5
Dudley Road 13 B3
Dudmore Road ..13 A3/37 D3
Dukes Close 7 A2
Dulverton Avenue 13 C4
Dumbarton Terrace 37 C5
Dummer Way 24 H2
Dunbar Road 18 E4
Dunbeath Court 7 A6
Dunbeath Road 7 A6
Duncan Street 29 B2
Dundas Close 25 A4
Dunedin Close 36 G6
Dunkirk Hill 25 B2
Dunley Close 5 B1
Dunnet Close 29 B2
Dunnington Road 33 A5
Dunraven Close 13 B5
Dunsford Close 11 D5
Dunster Close 13 A6
Dunwich Drive 11 B4
Durham Street 37 C4
Durnford Road 6 G2
Durrington Walk 6 G2
Dursden Lane 34 H4

Dyehouse Lane 25 D2/D3
Dyers Close 24 H1
Dykes Mews.................19 A5
E
Eagle Close 14 G2
Earl Close......................10 F2
East Court 24 E2
East Drive*, Blunsdon Abbey
Caravan Park..........1 B5
East Gate 32 H4
East Street 37 A3
Eastcott Hill..............37 B4/B5
Eastcott Road................37 B6
Eastern Avenue
(Chippenham) 22 G5/G6
Eastern Avenue (Swindon)
..............................13 A3
Easterton Lane.............34 G6
Eastfield Cottages 26 F3
Eastfield Villas 26 F3
Eastleaze Road 11 A3
Eastleigh Close 26 G5
Eastleigh Road..............26 G5
Eastmere 14 F6
Easton Lane 23 A4/B3
Eastrop..........................31 C4
Eastview Terrace 31 C3
Eastville Road 6 G4
Eastwood Avenue 33 B4
Eaton Close 13 C6
Eaton Wood 4 G5
Ebble Close 36 F4
Ebor Close 1 B6
Ebor Gardens................29 C6
Ebor Paddock................29 C6
Ecclestone Close 13 D6
Ecklington......................14 E4
Edale Moor....................14 G6
Edencroft 31 D1/D2
Edgar Row Close 18 E5
Edgehill 10 H6
Edgeware Road 37 B3
Edgeworth Close 11 A2
Edinburgh Street 6 H6
Edington Close..............10 H4
Edison Road..................14 F4
Edmund Street 37 B5
Edreds Court 29 C4
Edridge Close 22 G5
Edridge Place................35 C3
Edward Road 26 E5
Edwardian Court 34 G5
Edwards Meadow..........27 B4
Egerton Close 13 D2
Eider Avenue 34 G2
Elborough Road 5 B4
Elcombe Avenue 17 D5
Elcot Close 28 F4
Elcot Lane......................28 F4
Elcot Orchard 28 G4
Eldene Drive 14 E1/F3
Eldene Shopping Centre
..............................14 E5
Elder Close......................5 A4
Elder Court*, Lavender Drive
..............................29 B6
Elgin Drive 7 A6
Eliot Close 14 F6
Elizabeth Close..............28 F5
Elizabeth Drive 26 F3
Elizabeth House*, Dudley Rd.
..............................13 B4
Elizabeth Place 24 H3
Elizabeth Square 36 F5
Ellingdon Road..............17 D4
Elliott Court....................26 E6
Elm Close (Calne) 29 C6
Elm Close (Lyneham) ..34 G2
Elm Close (Wootton B.) 33 B1
Elm Cottages 8 G2
Elm Court (Devizes) 26 E6
Elm Court (Wootton B.) 33 B4
Elm Grove (Swindon)....10 G1
Elm Grove (Wootton B.) 35 B3
Elm Hayes 35 D5
Elm Park........................33 A4
Elm Road 6 E5
Elm Tree Close 26 G5
Elm Tree Gardens 26 G5
Elmer Close 32 G2
Elmina Road..................37 C2
Elmleaze Cottages........32 G6
Elmore......................14 E3/E4
Elms, The (Highworth) ..31 B4
Elms, The (Swindon) 10 F1
Elmswood Close.............7 A2
Elmswood Terrace 27 D3
Elmwood........................22 F3
Elsham Way 6 E2
Elsie Hazell Court 10 G5
Elsie Millin Court 6 G5
Elstree 6 E2
Elstree Way....1 C6/5 D1/6 E2
Ely Close 11 A5
Emerson Close................6 E1
Emery Gate Shopping Centre
..............................22 F6
Emery Lane 22 F6
Emlyn Square 12 F3
Emmanuel Close 6 E3
Emporium Court*,
Newport Street......12 H6
Enford Avenue 6 G1
Englefield 33 B4
Ensor Close 1 C5
Epsom Close 23 A1
Epworth Court 37 C6
Eric Long Court..............14 F5
Erin Court 12 E4
Erleigh Drive..................21 D6
Erlestoke Way 6 G1
Ermin Street 7 C3/C4
Erneston Crescent 35 B4
Ernle Road 29 C3
Escott Close..................24 G3
Eshton Walk..................13 C6
Esmead 22 F5
Espringham House..........7 A3
Espringham Place 7 A2
Essex Walk....................13 B3
Estcourt Crescent..........26 E3
Estcourt Hill 25 D4
Estcourt Street 26 E4
Estcourt Terrace*,
Estcourt Street 26 F3
Estcourt Villas*,
Estcourt Crescent 26 E3
Ethelred Place 35 B3
Euclid Street..................37 C4
Evans Close 22 F4
Eveleigh Road 33 B3
Evelyn Street 12 H6
Evergreens Close............8 E6
Everleigh Road (Pewsey)
..............................34 F6
Everleigh Road (Swindon)
..............................6 G2
Eworth Close 10 F4
Exbury Close 6 E1
Exe Close 6 E3
Exeter Close..................23 A2
Exeter Street 12 E3
Exmoor Close..................5 A3
Exmouth Street..............12 E4
F
Factory Cottages 7 A4
Fair View*, St. Michaels Av.
..............................31 B3
Fairfax Close 13 B2
Fairfield (Cricklade) 30 F3
Fairfield (Wootton B.) 33 B2
Fairfoot Close................21 B6
Fairford Crescent 6 G4/H3
Fairholm Way 7 B3
Fairlawn 14 F6
Fairview (Cricklade) 30 G3
Fairview (Swindon) 12 F4
Fairview*, Pool Gastons Rd.
..............................32 F3
Fairway*, Stockley La. ..29 D6
Falcon Road..................29 D4
Falconer Mews 6 F1
Falconscroft 14 E1
Falkirk Road 18 E4
Falkner Close 27 B5
Fallow Field Close 21 C3
Falmouth Grove 13 A5
Fanstones Road 14 E5
Faraday Park 14 G4
Faraday Road 14 G4/G5
Fareham Close..............13 D4
Farfield Lane 30 H6
Faringdon Road 12 E4
Farleigh Close 23 B1
Farleigh Crescent..........13 A6
Farleigh Place 25 C3
Farman Close................14 E5
Farmer Close 22 F4
Farmer Crescent 6 G1
Farmhouse Drive 24 G3
Farmhouse Lane 13 A2
Farnborough Road........13 D6
Farne Way 15 A1/33 D3
Farnsby Street 37 A4
Farrar Drive 27 A5
Farrfield 7 A3
Farriers Close................13 A1
Farthingale Cottages 35 B3
Feather Wood................11 B4
Fenland Close 10 F1
Fennel Close 5 B3
Ferguson Road 26 G6
Ferndale Road....11 D1/12 G1
Fernham Road 5 D4
Ferns, The 12 G1
Ferozeshah Road..........26 H1
Ferrers Drive..................10 F5
Fessey House 5 C3
Fiddle, The 30 E4
Field Rise 12 E6
Field View......................22 E6
Fieldfare 14 F2
Fields, The 7 C6
Figgins Lane..................27 D5
Figsbury Close 5 A2
Filands 32 G1
Filsham Road..................4 H1
Finchdale 14 F1
Firecrest View 14 G3
Firs, The*, Spinney Cl. ..23 B1
Firth Close 6 E4
Fitzmaurice Close..........14 F2
Fitzmaurice Square 29 C4
Fitzroy Road..................18 G1
Fitzwarren Close 24 H2
Five Alls Court 28 E4
Five Stiles Road 28 F5
Fleet Road 22 E5
Fleet Street....................37 A3
Fleetway House 37 A3
Fleetwood Court............10 G6
Fleming Way............37 A3/C3
Flint Hill..........................11 A5
Florence Street 12 G1
Foghamshire 22 E6
Folkestone Close 23 B1
Folkestone Road 37 A6
Folly Close 31 C2
Folly Crescent 31 C2
Folly Drive 31 C2
Folly Road 26 G1/G2
Folly Way 31 C2
Fonthill Walk..................13 B4
Ford Close 14 E5
Ford Street 12 E4
Fordson Road................26 F6
Forest Dale Road..........28 G5
Forest Drive 36 F6
Forest Hill Cottages 28 H6
Forest Lane.............24 F4/G2
Forest View 28 E4
Forester Close 14 F5
Forge Fields 9 D1
Forman Street 29 C4
Forrester Place 32 G2
Forsey Close 14 G2
Fortune Way 24 G2
Forty Acres Road 26 F4
Forty, The 30 F4
Forum Close..................14 E1
Forum, The....................11 A4
Fosse Close 11 D3
Fosseway Court*, Curtis St.
..............................12 F4
Foundry Lane 22 F5
Foundry Road................32 F3
Fovant Close 4 G6
Fowey 10 G6
Fox Brook......................33 C3
Fox Close 21 C3
Fox Croft Walk 24 G3
Fox Wood 11 B4
Foxbridge 14 F2
Foxglove Road 5 B2
Foxglove Way................29 B2
Foxgrove 21 B3
Foxhill Close....................5 D4
Foxley Close....................7 A3
Foxley Road 32 E5
Frampton Close 10 H3
Francklyn Acre*,
Lawrence Acre......27 D3
Francomes 5 C3
Frank Warman Court 7 D4
Frankland Road 10 E6
Frankton Gardens 7 D5
Fraser Close..................13 D2
Frays Garden*, Bath Road
..............................30 E3
Fredericks Avenue 21 A6
Freeman Road..............26 G4
Frees Avenue 27 A1
Frensham Way..............34 G4
Freshbrook Way............10 H5
Friars Close 12 F6
Friesian Close 10 G2
Friesland Close 10 G2
Frilford Drive....................7 C6
Frith Copse 4 G5
Fritillary Court................37 D3
Frobisher Drive 13 B3/B4
Frogwell 21 A5
Frogwell Park 21 B5
Frome Road 5 D3
Front Lane 1 D2
Fry Close 11 D5
Fuller Avenue 35 C3
Fuller Close 7 B2
Fullers Avenue 30 F3
Fullerton Walk 11 D5
Furlong Close..................5 C2
Furse Hill Road 36 H5
Furze Close 4 G5
Furze Hill Lane 25 B6
Furzehill 35 C4
Fyfield Avenue 6 G2
Fynamore Gardens 29 B5
Fynamore Place*,
Bryans Close Rd...29 B3
Fyne Close 4 H5
G
Gable Close (Swindon)....6 F1
Gables Close (Devizes) 26 G5
Gains Lane 26 E3
Gainsborough Avenue ..33 C2
Gainsborough Court......10 G4
Gainsborough Way 10 G4/G6
Gairlock Close 4 H5
Gales Close 22 G5
Gales Ground 28 F5
Galley Orchard..............30 G3
Galloway Close 10 G2
Galloway Road................5 A2
Galsworthy Close 14 F5
Galton Way 11 C1
Gambia Street 37 D3
Gamekeepers Close........1 B6
Gantlettdene 14 G3
Ganton Way 7 A6
Gardens, The (Rodbourne)
..............................6 E4
Gardens, The (Swindon) 7 A2
Garfield Close................14 E6
Garrard Way..................13 B1
Garraways 15 A1/33 D3
Garsington Drive 5 A1
Garson Road 6 F1
Garth Close 21 C3
Gartons Road 10 F2
Gas Lane 30 F3
Gascelyn Close 21 B6
Gason Hill Road 36 E3
Gastons Road (Chippenham)
..............................21 D5
Gastons Road (Malmesbury)
..............................32 F4
Gaveller Road 5 A1
Gaynor Close 6 E1
Gays Place 7 B3
Gayton Way 13 D1
George Close 29 C4
George Gay Gardens*,
Wolsely Avenue 13 B5
George Hall Court*,
Cavendish Sq. 13 C5
George Lane 27 D5
George Selman Gardens*,
Twyford Close 13 C3
George Street................12 E3
George Tweed Gardens
..............................10 G1
George VI Road 36 E4
Gerard Walk..................10 G3
Gibbs Close 14 G2
Gifford Road....................7 D4
Gilberts Hill School House
..............................37 B5
Giles Avenue 30 F4
Gilling Way 14 F3
Gilman Close 1 C5
Ginnel The*, New Park Street
..............................25 D3
Gipsy Lane (Chippenham)
..............................24 E1
Gipsy Lane (Swindon) ..13 A1
Gisborne Close 36 G6
Gladstone Road 22 E6
Gladstone Street 37 C1
Gladys Plumley Gardens
..............................12 H1
Glebe Farm Buildings ..28 G3
Glebe Place 31 C3
Glebe Road 33 A4
Glebe Way 35 C3
Glebe, The 29 C4
Glendale Drive 24 F1
Gleneagles Close..........22 G6
Glenmore Road 5 A2
Glenville Close 33 B5
Glenwood Close............18 G1
Glevum Close..................3 C2
Glevum Road 8 E6
Globe Street 37 B6
Gloucester Close 23 B1
Gloucester House..........13 B1
Gloucester Road 32 G4
Gloucester Street
(Malmesbury) 32 G4
Gloucester Street
(Swindon)..............37 A2

Glovers Court 32 F4
Goddard Avenue 12 F5
Goddard Court*, Cricklade St. 37 C6
Goddard House*, Commonweal Rd. 12 F6
Goddard Road 34 F5
Godolphin Close 10 F6
Godwin Court 12 H5
Godwin Road 7 D4
Gold View 11 D5
Goldborough Cottages ..15 A6
Goldcrest Walk 14 G2
Golding Avenue 27 A5
Goldney Avenue 21 D6
Goldney House 35 B4
Goldsborough Close 10 H3
Gooch Street 37 B2
Goodrich Court 11 A5
Goodwood Way 23 A2
Gordon Gardens 37 B3
Gordon Road 37 B4
Gore Close*, Hepworth Road 5 D1
Goughs Way 33 C3
Goulding Close 7 C5
Gower Close (Grange Park) 10 F4
Gower Close (Swindon) ..7 B5
Grafton Road 6 G2
Graham Street 37 C1/C2
Grailey Close 14 E5
Granary Close (Devizes) 26 G4
Granary Close (Swindon) 10 F1
Granary Road 26 G4
Grand Avenue 28 H6
Grand Trunk Road ..36 H1/H3
Grandison Close 10 G3
Grange Close 31 C4
Grange Drive 7 C6
Grange Park Way 10 F4
Granger Close 24 G3
Granham Close 27 D5
Granham Hill 27 D6
Grantham Close 10 H6
Grantley Close 13 C6
Granville Street 37 A4
Grasmere 14 G6
Graythwaite Close 5 D1
Great Western Road 25 D3
Great Western Way 10 E6/11 A6/37 B1
Green Drove 34 G6
Green Lane 26 E6
Green Meadow Avenue ..5 D3
Green Road 7 A4
Green Valley Avenue 5 D3
Green, The (Calne) 29 B4
Green, The (Highworth) 31 B4
Green, The (Lyneham) ..34 F1
Green, The (Marlborough) 28 E4
Green, The (Wootton B.) 15 A1/33 D3
Green, The*, Herd St. ..27 D4
Greenbridge Road 13 C2
Greenfield Road 26 E6
Greenfields 8 G2
Greenham Walk 13 D3
Greenhill Road 5 C5
Greenlands Road 7 A4
Greens Lane 18 F6
Greensand Close 1 B6
Greenway Avenue 22 E4
Greenway Close 13 D2
Greenway Court 22 E3
Greenway Drive 34 F3
Greenway Gardens 22 E4
Greenway Lane 22 E3
Greenway Park 22 E4
Greenway Road 28 H2
Greenwich Close 6 E2
Gresham Close 13 B3
Grey Road 28 F6
Greywethers Avenue 13 A6
Grierson Close 29 B4
Griffen Alley*, Cross Hayes La. ..32 G4
Griffiths Close 7 D6
Grindal Drive 10 F4
Grosmont Drive 10 H4
Grosvenor Road 12 E5
Groundwell Road 37 C4
Grove Cottages 1 A4
Grove Farm Cottages 1 A5
Grove Hill 31 B2
Grove Orchard 31 B2
Grove Road 35 C5
Grovelands Avenue 12 G6
Grovely Close*, Shearwood Road 4 G6
Groves Street 11 D3
Groves, The 6 F4
Grundys 14 F6
Guildford Avenue 13 B6
Gundry Close (Chippenham) 24 G2
Gundry Close (Devizes) 26 F3
Guppy Street 11 D2
Guthrie Close 29 C2
Guyers Lane 35 B2
Gypsy Patch 26 H2
H
Habrels Close 24 G1
Hackett Close 7 A3
Hackleton Rise 13 D1
Hackpen Close 18 F4
Haddon Close (Swindon) 10 F4
Haddons Close (Malmesbury) 32 E5
Hadleigh Close 11 A3
Hadleigh Rise 7 C2
Hadrians Close 8 E6
Haig Close 7 A3
Haines Terrace 34 F5
Half Way Firs*, Bath Road 35 B1
Halifax Close 18 E4
Hall Close 18 E5
Hallam Moor 20 G1
Hallsfield 30 E3
Ham Close 10 H4
Ham Cottages 15 A6
Hamble Road 5 D3
Hambleton Avenue 26 H1
Hamilton Close 13 B2
Hamilton Court 36 H4
Hamilton Drive 23 A2
Hamilton Green*, Hamilton Court 36 H4
Hamlet Court 22 F4
Hamlet, The 22 F4
Hammonds 30 G3
Hampshire Close*, Berkshire Drive 10 G2
Hampshire Cross 36 G5
Hampton Court*, Hampton Dr. 10 F3
Hampton Drive 10 F3
Hamstead Way 1 B6
Hamworthy Road 14 E3
Hanbury Road 13 B5
Hancock Close*, Crown Cl. 24 H2
Handel Street 12 H1
Hanks Close 32 G2
Hannington Close 6 F1
Hanover Court 14 F2
Hanover House 31 B4
Hanson Close 10 H1
Harber Court*, May Cl. 6 G5
Harbour Close 5 D4
Harcourt Road 12 E1
Hardbrook Court 21 D5
Hardenhuish Avenue 21 D4
Hardenhuish Lane 21 C4
Hardens Close 24 H2
Hardens Mead 24 H1
Hardhams Rise 35 C4
Hardie Close 7 C6
Harding Street 37 A3
Hardwick Close 6 E2
Hare & Hounds Street ..26 E4
Hare Close 7 B1
Harebell Close 5 B2
Harebell Way 26 G2
Hares Patch 21 C3
Harford Close 24 G2
Hargreaves Road 6 H1
Harlech Close 10 H5
Harlestone Road 13 D1
Harley Court*, London Road 28 E4
Harnish Way 21 C3
Harold Thorpe Gardens *, Middleton Close 13 B3
Harpers Lane 32 F4
Harptree Close 10 G1
Harriers, The 14 E2
Harrington Walk 13 B2
Harris Court*, The Strand 29 B4
Harris Road (Calne) 29 C1
Harris Road (Swindon) 6 E5
Harrow Close 7 B6
Harrow Grove 34 G2
Harry Edwards Court 13 B3
Harry Garrett Court*, Willow Walk 18 F5
Hartfield 25 C5
Hartham Lane 35 A4
Hartington Road 4 H1
Hartland Close 13 C4
Hartmoor Close 25 D5
Hartmoor Road 25 C6
Hartsthorn Close 5 B4
Harvester Close 10 F1
Harvey Grove 5 D5
Hastings Court 18 E5
Hastings Drive 34 H2
Hastings Road 35 C5
Hatch Road 7 D3
Hatchers Crescent 1 D3
Hatfield Close 5 C2
Hathaway Road 7 A2/A3
Hatherall Close 8 E5
Hatherell Road 24 G3
Hatherleigh Court*, Ringwood Close ..13 D3
Hatherley Road 13 D2
Hathersage Moor 20 G1
Hatton Grove 13 B3
Hatton Way 35 C3
Havelock Square 37 A4
Havelock Street 37 A4
Haven Close 13 D1
Hawfinch Close 14 G4
Hawker Road 14 E5
Hawkins Close 24 G2
Hawkins Court 18 E5
Hawkins Meadow 27 B5
Hawkins Street 11 D2
Hawkswood 14 F1
Hawksworth Way 12 E2
Hawthorn Avenue 6 G5
Hawthorn Close 34 G4
Hawthorn Road (Chippenham) 22 F4
Hawthorn Road (N. Tidworth) 36 F5
Hawthorns, The 32 E5
Hay Lane (Swindon) 10 F3/G4
Hay Lane (Wroughton) 16E1/F2/G4
Hay Lane Gypsy Caravan Site 16 F1
Haydock Close 23 A2
Haydon Court 5 C2
Haydon Court Drive 5 C2
Haydon End Lane 5 B1
Haydon Street 37 B2
Haydon View Road 6 G3
Haydonleigh Drive 5 C2
Hayle Road 11 D3
Haynes Close 14 E5
Haywain Close 6 G1
Hayward Close (Chippenham) 24 G2
Hayward Close (Swindon) 6 E1
Hazel Close 28 G5
Hazel Copse 23 A1
Hazel End 33 C4
Hazel Grove (Calne) 29 B5
Hazel Grove (Swindon) ..6 G4
Hazelbury Crescent 14 E2
Hazelmere Close 13 D5
Headlands Cottages*, Headlands Grove 6 H4
Headlands Grove 6 H4
Heath Way 13 D1
Heathcote Close 10 H1
Heather Way 29 C6
Heathfield 22 F3
Heaton Close 6 E1
Hector Road*, Filsham Road 5 A1
Heddington Close 6 F2
Hedge Row 24 H3
Hedgerow Close 14 E4
Hedges Close 7 D4
Helmsdale 5 D3
Helmsdale Walk 13 C5
Helston Road 13 C4
Henley Drive 31 C2
Henley Road 13 B5
Henman Close 6 E2
Henrietta Court*, The Weavers 12 H6
Henry Street 37 A3
Hepworth Road 5 D1
Herbert Harvey Court 14 E1
Herd Street 27 D4
Hereford Close 23 B2
Hereford Lawns 13 B6
Hermitage Lane 7 A4
Hermitage, The 37 D6
Heron Close 29 D4
Heron Way 23 A1
Heronbridge Close 11 A4
Heronscroft 14 F2
Hertford Close*, Lennox Dr. 13 B3
Hesketh Crescent 12 H6
Hewitt Close 14 E5
Hewlett Close 24 H2
Hexham Close (Chippenham) 23 A1
Hexham Close (Swindon) 10 H4
Heytsbury Gardens 10 F5
Heywood Close 6 F2
Hicks Close 18 E5
High Lawn 25 B3
High Mead 33 C3
High Street (Blunsdon) 1 D4
High Street (Calne) 29 B4
High Street (Chippenham) 22 E6
High Street (Chiseldon) 19 A5
High Street (Corsham) ..35 B5
High Street (Cricklade) 30 F4/G3
High Street (Devizes) 25 D4
High Street (Haydon Wick) 5 C3
High Street (Highworth) 31 C4
High Street (Malmesbury) 32 G4
High Street (Manton) 27 A5
High Street (Marlborough) 27 D5
High Street (Pewsey) 34 G5
High Street (Purton) 3 B3
High Street (Swindon) ..37 D6
High Street (Wootton B.) 33 B2
High Street (Wroughton) 18 E6
High View 28 G4
Highclere Avenue 13 B5
Highdown Way 1 C6
Highfold 33 C4
Highgrove Close 29 D4
Highland Close 10 G2
Highmoor Copse 4 G6
Highnam Close 7 C6
Highridge Close 3 A4
Highwood Close 5 B3
Highworth Court*, Westrop 31 B3
Highworth Road (S. Marston) 8 F1
Highworth Road (Strat. St. Margaret) 7 C3
Hill Close 6 E2
Hill Corner Road 21 D3
Hill Rise 22 E3/F3
Hill Top Avenue 36 E4
Hill View Cottages 36 H4
Hill View Road 8 E6
Hillary Close 6 G3
Hillcrest 32 H5
Hillcrest Close 12 E5
Hillcroft 29 C4
Hilliers Yard 27 D4
Hillingdon Road 13 D5
Hillmead Drive 4 H6/10 H1
Hillside 3 C3
Hillside Avenue 12 E5
Hillside Way 1 C4
Hillview 33 C3
Hillworth Gardens 25 D4
Hillworth Road 25 C5/D5
Hillyard Close 10 F5
Hilmarton Avenue 6 G2
Hinkson Close 1 B5
Hinton Street 12 H1
Hither Close 21 B5
Hither Springs 35 D4
Hobbes Close 32 F3
Hobbs Row*, Highworth Rd. 7 C3
Hobley Drive 7 C4
Hocketts Close 34 F1
Hodder Court 32 G4
Hodds Hill 4 H5
Hodge Close 26 G4
Hodge Lane 32 F3
Hodson Road 19 C6
Hoggs Lane 3 A3
Holbein Close 10 G4
Holbein Court 10 G4
Holbein Field 10 G5
Holbein Mews 10 G4
Holbein Place 10 G4
Holbein Square*, Holbein Wk. 10 G5
Holbein Walk 10 G5
Holbrook House 37 A2
Holbrook Way 37 A3
Holdcroft Close 2 E3
Holden Crescent*, Haywood Close 6 F1
Holford Rise*, Bremilham Rd. 32 F4

Holinshead Place 10 G4
Holland Close 24 H3
Holland Walk 13 A3
Holliday Close 6 E1
Hollinsmoor........20 F1
Hollow........27 A5
Holloway........32 G4/H4
Holloway Cottages*, Green Drove 34 G6
Holly Close (Calne) 29 C6
Holly Close (Pewsey)....34 G4
Holly Close (Swindon) 6 E5
Holly Tree Walk 34 G5
Hollybush Close 21 B3
Hollybush Lane 34 G4
Holmes Close........24 G3
Holmleigh 5 C3
Holmoak Court........12 H5
Holton House 35 B5
Holts Row........27 D5
Holway Cottages 12 F6
Home Close (Chiseldon) 19 A5
Home Close*, Newlands Rd. 35 B5
Home Farm 31 B3
Home Farm Close 28 H3
Home Ground (Cricklade) 30 E3
Home Ground (Wootton B.) 15 A1/33 D3
Homefield (Wootton B.) 33 C3
Homefields (Marlborough) 28 F5
Homefields Close 28 F5
Honey Garston........29 C3
Honeybone Walk 14 G2
Honeybrook Close*, Saxon Street 21 C5
Honeyhill........33 A4
Honeylight View 6 E1
Honeymead 29 C3
Honeysuckle Close (Chippenham) 21 C2
Honeysuckle Close*, Cornflower Road 5 B2
Honeysuckle Cottages ..28 H3
Honiton Road 13 D4
Hook Close 4 G5
Hook Street 9 A3/10 E4
Hooks Hill........3 B3
Hoopers Place 12 H5
Hopgood Close 26 H1
Hopkins Orchard........30 F4
Hopkins Road*, The Patchway 26 G4
Hopton Close 10 H6
Hopton Park*, London Road 26 F3
Hopton Road 26 G1
Horace Street........11 D2
Horcott Road 4 H5
Horder Mews 37 D6
Horham Crescent........13 C5
Hornbeam Court........6 F5
Hornsey Gardens........7 C2
Horse Fair Lane 30 G3
Horsebrook........29 C4
Horsebrook Park......29 B5/C5
Horsefair*, Foundry Rd. 32 G4
Horsell Close 33 B3
Horseshoe Crescent 4 G6
Horton Avenue 26 H1
Horton Road (Devizes)..26 H1
Horton Road (Swindon) ..7 A1
Howard Close........13 B3
Howard Court*, London Rd. 29 B5
Huddleston Close........12 H1
Hudson Road 32 F4
Hudson Way........6 E2
Hudswell Lane 35 D1
Hughenden Yard 27 D4
Hughes Close........27 A5
Hughes Street 11 C2
Hugo Drive 6 E1
Hulbert Close 35 C3
Humber Lane 36 H3
Humbolts Hold 24 F2
Hungerdown Lane 21 C6/23 B1
Hungerford Close 10 F2
Hungerford House 35 B3
Hungerford Road (Calne) 29 B2
Hungerford Road (Chippenham) 22 E4
Hunsdon Close........13 C3
Hunt Street........37 C5
Hunters Grove 6 F6
Huntingdon Way........23 A2
Huntley Close........13 B2
Hunts Hill 1 D3
Hunts Rise 8 E1
Huntsland........33 C3
Hurst Crescent........6 G4
Hyde Lane (Marlborough) 27 C4
Hyde Lane (Purton) 3 C3
Hyde Road (Blunsdon)....6 H1
Hyde Road (Swindon)7 A1/B2
Hyde, The........3 D3
Hylder Close........5 B3
Hysopp Close........5 A3
Hythe Road 37 A5
I
Icomb Close 11 A5
Idovers Drive 11 A5
Iffley Road 11 D1
Imber Walk 6 F1
Inglesham Road........6 G2
Ingram Street........32 G4
Inlands Close 34 F5
Inverary Road........18 E4
Ipswich Street 12 G1
Iron Peartree Farm Cottages 25 C1
Ironmonger Lane 27 D4
Ironstone Close 1 A6
Irston Way 10 H5
Irving Way 27 C5
Isambard Place*, Wellington Street..12 G2
Isbury Road 28 E5
Isis Close (Calne)........29 A2
Isis Close (Swindon)........6 E4
Island, The*, Nursteed Road 26 E4
Islandsmead 14 E3/E4
Islay Crescent........31 B3
Islington Street 37 B3
Ivy Cottages*, Ivy Rd.....22 E6
Ivy Field 35 B5
Ivy Lane (Blunsdon) 1 D3
Ivy Lane (Chippenham) 22 E6
Ivy Road........22 E6
Ivy Road Cottages*, Ivy Road 22 E6
Ivy Walk 29 B4
Ivyfield Court 22 E6
Ixworth Close 10 G2
J
Jack Thorne Close........4 G5
Jacksoms Lane 21 D1
Jackson Close 26 F5
Jacobs Walk 14 F5
Jagdalik Close*, Humber La. 36 H3
James Close 24 H3
James Watt Close 12 E2
James Wilkes House 5 C3
Jamrud Road 36 G3
Janbry Park Caravan Park 26 G6
Jargeau Court 35 C5
Jasmine Close (Calne)..29 C5
Jasmine Close (Chippenham) 21 B4
Jasmine Close (Swindon) 5 B3
Jasmine Cottages*, Highworth Road 8 F1
Jefferies Avenue 6 H5
Jefferies Close 27 B5
Jellalabad Barracks 36 H3
Jellalabad Terrace 36 G3
Jennings Street 11 D3
Jersey Park 10 H1
Jewel Close 10 F4
Jewels Ash........3 C2
Jim Masters Court 6 G6
John Betjeman Close....32 G2
John Herring Crescent 7 C6
John Rennie Close........25 C5
John Rumble Close 26 F4
John Street........37 A3
Joiner Lane 37 C6
Jole Close........7 A2
Jolliffe Street........12 E4
Jordan Close 24 G2
Joseph Street*, Albion Street 12 E4
Joyce Close 1 C6
Jubilee Buildings 25 D3
Jubilee Court 36 F4
Jubilee Estate........3 B2
Jubilee Gardens 32 F3
Jubilee Road (Devizes) 26 G4
Jubilee Road (Swindon) ..5 B4
Juliana Close 10 G2
Jump Farm Road 26 F4
Juniper Close 13 D1
Juniper Court 36 F6
Juno Way 11 D5
K
Karachi Close........36 E3
Karslake Close 14 E5
Katifer Lane 32 G4
Keats Close 33 C2
Keats Crescent........7 B3
Keble Close 14 E2
Keels 30 E2
Keevil Avenue 29 A4
Kelham Close........13 B5
Kelham Gardens 28 E4
Kellsboro Road........17 D4
Kelly Gardens........5 D1
Kelmscot Road........6 G4
Kelso Court........23 A2
Kelvin Road 13 C2
Kemble Drive 12 E2
Kembles Close*, Swindon Rd. 32 H5
Kembrey Street 6 H5
Kemerton Walk........13 D6
Kemp Close 26 F3
Kempsfield 26 F6
Kempsters Court 3 C3
Kempton Park Court*, Aintree Drive 23 A1
Kendal 10 H5
Kenilworth Lawns 13 B6
Kennedy Drive........14 F4/F5
Kennet Avenue 6 F3
Kennet Court*, High St. 27 D5
Kennet House........12 E6
Kennet Mews*, Angel Yard 27 D4
Kennet Place 27 D4
Kennet Road (Devizes) 26 F5
Kennet Road (N. Tidworth) 36 F5/G5
Kennet Road (Wroughton) 18 E4
Kennet Walk........29 A2
Kensington Way 21 A6
Kent Close 23 B1
Kent Road 37 A5/A6
Kenton Close 13 D3
Kenwin Close 7 D4
Kerrs Way........18 E5
Kerry Close 10 G2
Kerry Crescent*, New Road 29 B4
Kershaw Road 14 E5
Kessingland Court*, Bath Rd. 12 F5
Kestrel Drive 14 G3
Keswick Road 13 D6
Keycroft Copse 4 F6
Keyneston Road........14 E3
Keynsham Walk 13 D5
Kibblewhite Close........3 B4
Kilben Close 10 F2
Kilda Road 31 A2
Kiln Close........26 G4
Kiln Lane 5 D6
Kilns, The 29 C2
Kilsby Drive 13 D1
Kilsyth Close 10 G5
Kilverts Close 23 B1
Kimberley Road 13 B5
Kimbolton Close........10 G5
Kimmeridge Close 13 D3
King Alfred Close 34 G5
King Alfred Street........21 D5
King Charles Road........10 H5
King Henry Drive (Chippenham)......24 H3
King Henry Drive (Swindon)........10 F5
King John Street........37 C6
King Street 37 A3
King William Street........37 B6
Kingfisher Drive (Devizes) 26 H2
Kingfisher Drive (Swindon) 14 F2
Kingham Close........21 D6
Kings Avenue (Chippenham) 23 A1
Kings Avenue (Corsham) 35 A4
Kings Avenue (Highworth) 31 C4
Kings Corner 34 G5
Kings Court 19 A5/20 E6
Kings Wall 32 G4
Kingsbury Square........27 D4
Kingsbury Street (Calne) 29 B4
Kingsbury Street (Marlborough) 27 D4
Kingsbury Terrace*, Kingsbury Street ..27 D4
Kingscote Close 10 F1
Kingsdown Lane (Blunsdon) 2 E5/H6
Kingsdown Lane (Swindon) 6 E4
Kingsdown Mobile Home Park 7 B1
Kingsdown Road 7 B2
Kingshill Court 12 E5
Kingshill Road 37 A6
Kingsley Avenue........33 B2
Kingsley Gardens 26 F4
Kingsley Road (Chippenham) 23 C1
Kingsley Road (Devizes) 26 F4
Kingsley Way 6 H2
Kingsmanor Wharf 26 G2
Kingsthorpe Grove 14 E1
Kingston Road 13 C5
Kingsway Close 13 C5
Kingswood Avenue 13 C4
Kipling Gardens 7 A3
Kirby Close (Devizes) ..26 G3
Kirby Close (Swindon) ..13 B5
Kirby Road 35 B3
Kirkee Road 36 G3
Kirkstall Close........11 A5
Kirktonhill Road 11 B3
Kishorn Close........4 H5
Kitchener Street 6 G6
Kitefield........30 F3
Knapp Close*, Cheney Manor Rd...6 E5
Knapp, The........29 C4
Knight Close........24 G3
Knoll, The*, Croft Rd. 12 G6
Knolton Walk*, Priory Road 13 C5
Knowlands 31 C2
Knowle, The (Corsham) 35 C4
Knowle, The*, Stockley Lane 29 C6
Knowsley Road 13 C5
Kohat Close 36 F3
L
Laburnam Drive 33 B2
Laburnum Road 6 G4
Lacemakers Road 32 G2
Lackham Circus 23 C1
Lacock Road (Corsham) 35 C5
Lacock Road (Swindon)..6 G3
Ladbrook Lane 35 D6
Ladds Lane........24 F1
Lady Coventry Road 22 G6
Lady Godley Close........36 G4
Lady Lane 1 B6/C5/5 D1
Lady Mead 30 F3
Ladydown........29 B3
Ladyfield Road....21 C6/23 C1
Laggar, The 35 A4
Lagos Street........37 B2
Lahore Close 36 E3
Lahore Road 36 G4
Laines Head........21 D3
Laineys Close........27 D3
Lakeside........13 A6
Lambert Close 10 H6
Lamberts 21 B5
Lambourn Avenue 13 A6
Lamora Close 10 F1
Lampeter Road........5 A1
Lanac Road 7 C6
Lancaster Mews 8 E1
Lancaster Place 8 E1
Lancaster Road 18 E5
Lancaster Square........34 G2
Lancefield Place........35 B3
Landor Road........1 B5
Langdale Drive........10 H6
Langford Grove 13 A3
Langley Court 22 F5
Langley Road (Chippenham) 22 F4
Langley Road (Swindon) 4 H6
Langport Close........10 G5
Langstone Way 11 A3
Lanhill View 21 C3
Lanhydrock Close 10 G5
Lansbury Drive 7 B3
Lansdown Grove 22 F4
Lansdown Place*, Blowhorn Street 28 E4
Lansdown Road 37 A6
Lansdowne Close........29 A2
Lansdowne Court*, Long St. 26 E4
Lansdowne Grove*, Sheep Street 26 E4
Lansdowne Square 29 A3
Lansdowne Terrace*, Morris Lane 26 E4
Lapwing Close 14 G3
Lapwing Crescent 21 C3

Larchmore Close 6 E4
Larkham Rise................24 G1
Larksfield 14 E1
Latton Close 6 F1
Laughton Way 6 E1
Laurel Court 7 A4
Laurel Drive 28 F5
Lavender Drive..............29 B5
Lawn Cottages*, The Planks 12 H5
Lawn Lane 2 H1
Lawns, The....................33 A3
Lawrence Acre 27 D3
Lawrence Close (Devizes) 26 E6
Lawrence Close (Swindon) 14 E5
Lawton Close 13 C6
Le Marchant Close........26 G2
Lea Close........................1 C6
Leaf Close 28 E4
Leamington Grove 19 A1
Leaze Road 27 C3
Lechlade Road..............31 C3
Legate Close*, Roman Way 24 H2
Leicester Street 37 C4
Leigh Road......................6 F3
Leighton Avenue 13 B5
Leland Close 32 G2
Lennox Drive...........13 A3/B3
Lenton Close 21 A6
Leonora Home*, Wood Lane 24 G1
Les Gowing House*, Milston Avenue 6 F2
Lesley Anne Skeete Court 13 D5
Lesley Court..................37 A5
Leslie Close 10 G5
Lethbridge Road 12 G6
Letterage Road 4 G5
Leven 10 G6
Leverton Gate................19 B2
Lewis Close 5 D1
Lewisham Close..............5 D4
Lichen Close....................5 B3
Lickhill Road 29 A1/A2
Liddington Street 6 G4
Liden Drive 14 E6/F5/20 F1
Light Close 35 A5
Lilac Court 6 F5
Lilac Way 29 B5
Lilian Lock Gardens*, Everleigh Road 6 G2
Lime Close (Lyneham)..34 H2
Lime Close (Pewsey)....34 G4
Lime Kiln........................33 B2
Lime Tree Close*, Long Barrow Rd. ..29 A4
Limes Avenue..................6 F4
Lincoln Street 37 C4
Lindas View 33 C1
Linden Avenue 6 G4
Linden Close (Calne) 29 B5
Linden Close (Wootton B.) 33 B2
Linden Court..................37 A3
Linden Way 4 G5
Lindisfarne 33 D2
Lindley Close 36 G5
Lineacre Close 10 F5
Lingfield Close*, Hamilton Dr. 23 A1
Link Avenue 10 H4
Links, The......................34 F5
Linley Close 18 G1
Linley Road 2 E4
Linnetsdene 14 E1
Linslade Street 11 D3
Liskeard Way 10 H5
Lisle Close 10 G4
Lismore Road 31 A2
Lister Road 18 F4
Little Avenue....................6 E6
Little Brittox 25 D3
Little Court*, The Weavers 12 H5
Little Down 21 C6
Little Englands*, Wood Lane 24 F1
Little Island 34 E5
Little London..................37 C6
Little London Court........37 C6
Little Park Close 34 F3
Little Rose Lane 1 C1
Littlecote 21 B6
Littlecote Close..............11 B4
Littlecote Road 23 B1
Locks Lane 3 B2
Locks, The 25 B3
Locksgreen Crescent 5 C3
Lockside........................24 G2
Lockswell Close 24 H3
Lodge Close*, Long Barrow Rd. ..29 A4
Lodge Hardenhuish Avenue 21 D5
Lodge Road 24 G2
Logan Close 13 A3
Lombard Court 10 H5
Lomond Close 4 H5
London Road (Calne) 29 B5
London Road (Chippenham) 24 F1/H1
London Road (Devizes) 26 F3
London Road (Marlborough) 28 E4
London Street................12 F3
Long Acre........................3 B3
Long Barrow Road 29 A4
Long Close (Chippenham) 24 G1
Long Close (Liddington) 20 H4
Long Harry 28 F6
Long Ridings 21 D3
Long Street....................26 E4
Longcroft Avenue 26 F4
Longcroft Cottages*, Nursteed Road......26 F4
Longcroft Cresent..........26 F4
Longcroft Road..............26 F4
Longfellow Close 1 C5
Longfellow Cresent 33 C2
Longfields Walk 26 F5
Longleat Gardens 6 G3
Longleaze......................33 B2
Longleys Close..............26 H5
Longs Buildings*, New Park Street ..25 D3
Longstock Court 10 H3
Longstone Road 21 B4
Longthorpe Close..........11 B5
Lonsdale Close................2 E4
Loop Road 28 H6
Lords Lane 22 F6
Lords Mead 21 B5
Lorne Street 12 E4
Lotmead Cottages ..14 G2/H2
Loughborough Close 10 F5
Louviers Way 18 G1
Loveage Close 5 B3
Lovell Close 14 F2
Loveridge Close 7 A1
Lovers Lane 32 G3
Lovers Walk*, The Bridge 22 E6
Loves Cottages 13 D6
Low Lane 29 C5
Lowa Road....................36 G3
Lowden..........................23 D1
Lowden Avenue 21 D5
Lowden Hill....................21 D6
Lower Church Fields 27 D5
Lower Lodge Cottages ..24 F4
Lower Prospect*, Blowhorn Street 28 E4
Lower Salthrop Farm Cotts. 16 G4
Lower Wharf..................25 D3
Lower Widhill Farm Cottages 1 A2
Lowes Close....................4 H5
Loxley Walk 13 D6
Loyalty Street 21 D6
Lucerne Close (Swindon) 10 F1
Lucerne Close (Wootton B.) 33 A1
Luckett Way 29 B2
Lucknow Barracks 36 G3
Luddesdown Road 11 A5
Ludgershall Road (N. Tidworth) 36 F5
Ludgershall Road (Swindon) 11 C5
Ludlow Close (Chippenham) 24 H2
Ludlow Close (Swindon)13 A5
Ludmead Road..............35 D5
Lukas Close 1 B6
Lulworth Road 5 C4
Lumley Close 10 F5
Lupin Court......................7 A4
Lutyens Gate 19 B2
Lyall Close 1 A5
Lyddon Way 5 D3
Lydford Close................10 G1
Lydiard Green..................3 A6
Lydiard Residential Caravan Park 9 B3
Lydiard Road 23 B1
Lyme Way 6 E2
Lyndhurst Crescent 13 C3/C4
Lyneham Close................6 F1
Lynmouth Road 11 D3
Lynton Road....................5 C6
Lynwood Grove 5 B4
Lypiatt Mead..................35 D5
Lypiatt Road 35 D5
Lysley Close..................24 H2
Lytchett Way..................14 E3
Lytham Close 22 G6
M
MacAulay Square..........29 C4
Mackenzie Close 14 F5
Macklin Court 27 D5
Macneice Drive..............27 A5
Macs Yard 24 F1
Magnolia Court 6 F5
Magnolia Rise................29 B5
Magpie Lane 14 G3
Magpie Mews*, Bridewell St. 26 E4
Maidstone Road 37 A6
Main Drive*, Blunsdon Abbey Caravan Park..........1 B5
Maitland Close 24 H2
Maitland Road 13 C2
Majestic Close 10 G2
Maldwyn Close 10 F2
Mall, The (N. Tidworth)..36 H1
Mall, The (Swindon) 12 F5/F6
Mallard Avenue 34 G2
Mallard Close (Calne) ..29 D4
Mallard Close (Devizes) 26 H1
Mallard Close (Swindon) 14 G3
Mallow Close 5 A3
Malmesbury Road ..21 D1/D2
Malmesbury House........36 F5
Malthouse Close..............2 E3
Malthouse Flats 35 B5
Maltings, The (Malmesbury) 32 G4
Maltings, The (Wootton B.) 33 A4
Malvern Road..................6 G6
Manchester Road..........37 B2
Mannington Court*, Raybrook Cres. 11 C2
Mannington House 11 B4
Mannington Lane 11 B4
Mannington Park 11 D2
Manor Bridge Court 36 E4
Manor Close (Swindon) ..2 E3
Manor Close (Wroughton) 18 F6
Manor Cottages (Malmesbury)........32 H5
Manor Cottages (Swindon) 8 H3
Manor Court 34 F6
Manor Crescent 5 D5
Manor Farm Cottages ..25 A1
Manor Farm Lane 8 G4
Manor Gardens 5 D6
Manor Meadows*, Manor Pk. 8 G3
Manor Mews..................34 F6
Manor Orchard..............30 G3
Manor Park 8 G3
Manor Road (Calne)......35 A4
Manor Road (Chippenham) 21 B5
Manor Road (Swindon) 11 D4
Manor View 19 A5
Manse, The*, Kennet Place 27 D4
Manton 27 A5
Manton Close 27 A6
Manton Drove................27 A6
Manton Hollow 27 A5
Manton Street................11 D2
Maple Close (Calne)......29 B6
Maple Close (Pewsey) ..34 G4
Maple Drive 33 B2
Maple Grove 6 G5
Maple Terrace 36 F6
Maple Way 22 E3
March Close....................5 D1
Mardale Close 4 F6
Marden Court*, Quarr Barton 29 B4
Marden Way..................29 A5
Margaret Leckie Court ..13 A3
Margaret Matthews Court 11 C2
Marigold Close 5 B3
Marina Close (Devizes) 26 H1
Marine Close (Wroughton) 18 F4
Marjoram Close 5 B2
Markenfield....................11 B5
Market Cross 32 G4
Market Hill 29 B4
Market Lane*, Oxford Street 32 G4
Market Place (Chippenham) 22 F6
Market Place (Pewsey) 34 G5
Market Place*, High Street 31 C4
Market Place, The (Devizes) 25 D4
Market Street 37 A4
Markham Close 13 B2
Markham Place 18 E5
Markham Road..............18 E6
Marlborough Close*, Horton Road 26 H1
Marlborough Court (Chippenham) 21 C6
Marlborough Court*, Shakespeare Rd...33 C2
Marlborough House 12 E5
Marlborough Lane 12 H6
Marlborough Road (Chiseldon) 19 B5
Marlborough Road (Pewsey) 34 F4
Marlborough Road (Swindon) ..12 H5/19 A1
Marlborough Road (Wootton B.)..........33 B5
Marlborough Road (Wroughton)..........18 F6
Marlborough Street........12 E4
Marlowe Avenue............13 B2
Marlowe Way 33 C2
Marney Road 10 G4
Marsh Farm Lane..........13 A2
Marsh, The....................20 H1
Marshall Road (Devizes) 26 G6
Marshall Road (Swindon) 10 H1
Marshall Street..............21 D6
Marshfield Cottages 1 A2
Marshfield Road............21 D5
Marshfield Way 7 C5
Marshgate 13 B1
Marsland Road................6 H4
Marston Avenue..............6 H3
Martin Way....................29 D4
Martinfield......................14 F2
Martins Close 22 H5
Martinsell Green............34 G4
Maryport Street..............26 E4
Masefield 33 C2
Masefield Avenue............7 A4
Maskeleyne Way 17 D4
Maslen Close 26 G4
Maslin Row*, Delamere Drive 7 C3
Mason Road 6 F1
Masons Way 35 C2
Masons, The....................3 A4
Massey Close................24 F2
Massey Road................26 G6
Massinger Walk 13 B3
Matford Hill....................22 H5
Matilda Way..................26 G2
Matley Moor 20 G1
Mattock Close................26 F3
Maud Close 26 G3
Maud Heath Court 22 F5
Maud Heaths Causeway 22 F3/G2
Maundrell Road 29 C1
Maunsell Way................17 D4
Maur Close....................21 D6
Maxey Close 10 H1
Maxwell Street 12 E3
May Close 6 G5
Mayenne Place..............25 A4
Mays Lane 19 A6
Mayfield 28 E4
Mayfield Close 13 D2
Mayo Close 35 B3
Mayze House*, Mead Way 11 B2
Mead Way ..4 H6/10 H1/11 A2
Meadland 35 B3
Meadow Close (Chippenham) 21 B6
Meadow Close (Wootton B.) 33 B2
Meadow Court 36 E5
Meadow Drive................26 F3
Meadow Road 11 C2
Meadow Springs 9 D1
Meadow View*, Elcot Lane 28 G4
Meadow View*, Stockley La. 29 D6
Meadow Way 20 G4/G5
Meadowcroft 7 A3/B4
Meadows, The (Hook) 9 A4

Meadows, The (Malmesbury) 32 G2
Meadowsweet Close 5 C2
Meares Drive 10 H1
Medbourne Lane 20 H5
Medgbury Place 37 C3
Medgbury Road 37 C3
Medina Way 7 B3
Medlar Court 6 F5
Medway Road 5 D3
Meerut Road 36 G4
Melbourne Close 13 B6
Melbourne Mews*, The Nursery 25 C3
Melbourne Place*, The Nursery 25 C3
Melford Walk 14 E2
Melfort Close 4 H5
Melksham Close 6 F1
Melksham House*, Wylye Rd. 36 F4
Melksham Road 23 C3
Mellion Close 24 G1
Mellow Ground 5 C2
Melrose Close 11 A3
Melsome Road 34 F3
Melville Close 13 B3
Mendip Close 6 G4
Menham Close 6 H5
Mere Close 13 D5
Meriden Walk 13 D5
Meriton Avenue 35 B5
Merlin Cottages 28 E4
Merlin Court 27 C3
Merlin Way 14 F1/G2
Merrivale Grove 13 A5
Merton Avenue 6 H4
Merton Street 37 B3
Mervyn Webb Place 12 H1
Methuen Park 23 B2
Methuen Way 35 A4
Mews, The (Devizes) 26 E4
Mews, The (Highworth) 31 C3
Mews, The (Lydiard Millicent) 9 D1
Mews, The (Malmesbury) 32 F4
Mews, The*, Cricklade Street 12 H5
Meynell Close 1 B5
Michael Pyms Road 32 G2
Middi Haines Court 31 C3
Middle Field Close 26 F4
Middle Ground (Cricklade) 30 E3
Middle Ground (Wootton B.) 15 A1/33 D3
Middle Lodge Cottages 24 G4
Middleleaze Drive 10 F2
Middlemass Green 34 G5
Middleton Close 13 B3
Middlewick Lane 35 A3
Midhurst Avenue 13 D4
Midwinter Close 4 H5
Midwinter Gardens 7 C5
Mildenhall Way 6 F1
Mildmay Close 10 F4
Milestone 22 E3
Milestone Way 21 D3
Milford Street 37 A3
Milford Way 24 G3
Militia Court*, High Street 27 D5
Milk Marketing Board Cotts. 21 D1
Mill Close (Chiseldon) ..19 B5
Mill Close (Devizes) 26 F6
Mill Close (Wroughton)..18 F5
Mill Court 18 F6
Mill Hill Avenue 36 E4
Mill Lane (Malmesbury) 32 G4
Mill Lane (Swindon) 11 D6/17 C2
Mill Path 36 E2
Mill Road 26 F5
Mill Street 29 B4
Milland Cose 6 F1
Millard Close 24 G3
Millbuck Close 7 A6
Millenium Close*, Brickley La. 26 G4
Millennium Court 34 F5
Miller Close 10 F1
Milston Avenue 6 G2
Milton Road (Pewsey) ..34 H5
Milton Road (Swindon) ..12 F3
Miltons Way 33 A4
Milverton Court 13 C4
Minerva House*, Welton Rd. 11 B3
Minety Road 6 F2
Minster Close 1 B6
Minster Way 23 B2
Mint Close 5 B3
Minton Place 37 A2
Moat Walk 18 F6
Moffat Rise 32 G2
Monday Market Street ..26 E3
Monet Close 5 D1
Monks Close 36 F4
Monks Way 24 H3
Monkton Close 13 D5
Monkton Hill 22 E6
Monmouth Close 13 B6
Montagu Street 11 D2
Montague Close 22 H5
Monteagle Close 10 G5
Montgomery Avenue 6 F5
Montgomery House*, Sidbury Circ. Rd. ..36 E4
Montrose Close 5 C5
Monument Cottages*, Monument Hill 26 H6
Monument Hill 26 H6
Mooltan Barracks 36 F3
Moonrakers 26 G2
Moore Close 18 G3
Moorhen Close 14 G4
Moorlands 22 F3
Moorlands, The 25 D5
Moormead Road 18 F5
Moors, The 3 D6
Mopes Lane 3 B1
Moray Road 7 A6
Moredon Park 5 B4
Moredon Road 5 C4
Moresby Close 11 A3
Morie Close 4 H6
Morley Street 37 B4
Morning Rise 28 F4
Morris Lane 26 E4
Morris Road 27 B5
Morris Street 11 C3
Morrison Street 11 D2
Morse Close (Chippenham) 24 F3
Morse Close (Malmesbury) 32 G3
Morse Street 37 A5
Morstone Road 33 A5
Mortimer Close 10 H2
Moscow Mansions*, Dowling Street 12 G4
Moss Road 21 A5
Mount Pleasant (Marlborough) 28 E4
Mount Pleasant (Wootton B.) 33 A4
Mount Pleasant*, Bristol Rd. 21 B4
Mount View 32 H5
Mountbatten House*, Wingate Parade 6 E5
Mountings, The 18 F3
Moxhams*, Newlands Road 35 B5
Moyne Close 25 C3
Mud Lane 3 A5
Mulberry Close 21 C4
Mulberry Grove 6 E5
Mulberrys The*, Station Rd. 33 A3
Mulcaster Avenue 10 F4
Mundens Close 32 G4
Mundy Avenue 14 E5
Munro Close 13 A3
Murdock Road 14 G3
Murrayfield 22 F4
Muscovey Close 34 G2
Myrtle Gardens 6 G5
N
Nadder Road 36 G5
Nags Head Court*, New Park Street ..25 D3
Nantwich 10 G6
Napier Close (N. Tidworth) 36 F6
Napier Close (Swindon) 12 E2
Nash Close 1 C5
Naughton Avenue 26 H1
Naunton Road 13 C3
Neale Court 35 B4
Neate Road 26 G3
Neates Yard 27 D4
Neeld Crescent 21 C5
Nelson Street 11 D4
Nepaul Road 36 F4
Ness Close 4 H5
Nestleton Close 29 B5
Nether Leaze 34 E5
Netherton Close 13 D5
Nevis Close 4 H5
New Road 29 B4
New Bridge Close 37 B2
New Bridge Square 37 B2
New Bungalows 21 C5
New Cottages (Calne) ..29 D1
New Cottages (Chippenham) 21 A5
New Cottages (Hodson) 19 C6
New Cottages (Liddington) 20 H5
New Houses*, The Quadrangle 23 D1
New Park Road 26 E3
New Park Street 25 D3
New Place 35 B5
New Road (Chippenham) 22 E5
New Road (Chiseldon) ..19 A6
New Road (Marlborough) 27 D4
New Road (Purton) 3 B1
New Road (Wootton B.) 33 A4
Newall Tuck Road 22 G6
Newark Close 10 H6
Newburgh House 31 B3
Newburgh Place 31 B3
Newburn Crescent 11 D4
Newbury Avenue 29 A2
Newbury Drive (Chippenham) 23 A2
Newbury Drive (Swindon) 10 H6
Newby Acre 27 D3
Newcastle Street 37 C3
Newcombe Drive 12 E1
Newcroft Close 29 B2
Newcroft Road 29 B2
Newhall Street 37 A5
Newland Road (Swindon) 6 E4
Newlands Road (Corsham) 35 B5
Newlands Villas 1 B2
Newlands Walk*, Alan Cobham Rd. 26 G5
Newlands*, Kings Wall..32 G4
Newmarket Close 23 A1
Newmeadow Copse 4 G6
Newnton Grove 32 E3
Newport Street 12 H6
Newstead Close 5 D1
Newton Abbot Close 23 A1
Newton Way 6 G3
Niebull Close 32 G2
Nightingale Cottages 19 C3
Nightingale Lane 8 H3
Nightwood Copse 4 G5
Nindum Road 7 D6
Nolan Close 1 B5
Norbury Court 3 C3
Norcliffe Road 13 D5
Nore Marsh Road 33 B4
Noredown Way 33 C4
Norfolk Close 13 B3
Norman Close 24 H3
Norman Road 12 G1
Norris Close 19 A6
North Bank Rise 33 C3
North Cote 29 A3
North Drive*, Blunsdon Abbey Caravan Park 1 B5
North End 29 A2
North Leaze Close 5 D4
North Leaze Farm Cottages*, Lechlade Road 31 C3
North Meadow Road 30 E3
North Star Avenue 37 A1
North Street (Calne) 29 B3
North Street (Pewsey) ..34 F5
North Street (Swindon)..37 B5
North View 31 B4
North View House 3 B4
North View Place 27 D3
North Walk 35 A5
North Wall 30 F3
North Way 29 A3
Northampton Street 37 D3
Northbourne Road 1 C6
Northbrook Road 6 E6
Northern Road 6 E5/12 E1
Northfield Way 13 D1
Northfields 29 A3
Northgate Gardens 25 D3
Northgate Street 25 D3
Northleaze Mobile Home Park 35 B2
Northwood 22 F3
Norton Grove 37 D4
Norwood Close 14 F5
Noyes Close (Swindon) ..5 A2
Noyes Close (Chippenham) 21 A5
Nuffield Close 10 H1
Nuns Walk 32 G4
Nurseries, The (Swindon) 12 F5
Nursery Gardens 35 C5
Nursery, The (Devizes) 25 C3
Nursteed Close 26 G5
Nursteed Park 26 F5
Nursteed Place 26 H6
Nursteed Road 26 F4
Nuthatch Close 14 G3
Nutmeg Close 5 B3
Nyland Road 14 E2
Nythe Road 7 D6
O
O'Donnell 22 F3
Oak Close 36 F6
Oak Drive 31 B4
Oak Garden 7 C3
Oak Lodge Close 21 D5
Oak Road 23 A1
Oak Tree Avenue 6 H4
Oakford Walk 13 C3
Oakham Close 11 A5
Oakhurst Way 5 A1
Oakie Close 6 E2
Oaklands 22 E3
Oakleigh Terrace 3 C3
Oaks, The (Chippenham) 22 E3
Oaks, The*, Fox Brook..33 C3
Oaksey Road 6 G3
Oakwood Road 11 A2
Oamaru Way 26 G4
Oasthouse Close 10 G1
Oate Hill 24 G1
Oathills 35 C4
Oberon Way 6 E2
Ockwells*, The Forty 30 F4
Ocotal Way 13 A1/37 D1
Odcroft Close 22 G6
Odstock Road 6 G1
Offers Court 26 E4
Ogilvie Square 29 C3
Okebourne Park 14 E6
Okeford Close 14 E2
Okus Grove 6 H3
Okus Road 11 D6/37 A6
Old Alexander Road 32 E3
Old Cottages 20 H5
Old Court 33 B4
Old Ford Court*, High Street 34 G5
Old Hardenhuish Lane ..21 C4
Old Hospital Road 34 E4
Old Lion Court*, High Street 27 D5
Old Malmesbury Gardens 33 B1
Old Malmesbury Road ..33 B1
Old Mill Lane 12 H6
Old Orchard, The 32 G2
Old Park Farm Cotts. 25 B6
Old Park*, Furze Hill La.25 C6
Old Railway Close 32 G2
Old Road 22 E5
Old School Yard, The....35 C5
Old Shaw Lane 10 F1/G1
Old Swan Yard 26 E4
Old Town Court 37 C6
Old Vicarage Lane 8 G3
Old Yard, The 28 E5
Oldbury Prior 29 C6
Oldbury Way 29 A4
Oldlands Walk 13 D6
Olive Court 18 E6
Olive Grove 6 F4
Oliver Avenue 35 B4
Oliver Close 10 F3
Olivers Lane 32 G4
Olivier Road 6 F1
Omdurman Street 6 F6
Orange Close 31 C3
Orchard Close (Calne) ..29 C5
Orchard Close (Devizes) 26 E6
Orchard Close*, London Rd. 28 E4
Orchard Cottages 23 D6
Orchard Court (Malmesbury) 32 G5
Orchard Court (Swindon) 7 C6
Orchard Crescent 21 C6
Orchard Gardens 3 A4
Orchard Grove 6 H4
Orchard House*, Orchard Rd. 35 A4
Orchard Mead 15 A1/33 D3
Orchard Park 33 A4
Orchard Road (Chippenham) 21 C6
Orchard Road (Corsham) 35 A4
Orchard Road (Marlborough) 28 E5

Orchard, The 19 B2
Orchid Close 6 G4
Ordnance Road 36 F4
Orkney Close 10 H2
Orlando Close................10 F4
Orrin Close 4 H6
Orwell Close (Malmesbury)
............................32 G2
Orwell Close (Swindon) ..6 E2
Osborne Street..............12 F1
Osmund Close 26 G5
Osmund Road 26 G5
Osprey Close 14 G3
Osterley Road 5 C1
Otter Way......................33 C3
Oval Dean*, Bulford Rd.36 H4
Overbrook 14 E5/E6
Overton Gardens 7 D5
Overtown Hill 18 G6
Owl Close......................14 G3
Owlets, The 14 G3
Oxford Court*, Oxford Road
.............................29 B3
Oxford Road (Calne)29 B3/C3
Oxford Road (Swindon)
..........................7 C6/D6
Oxford Street (Malmesbury)
............................32 G4
Oxford Street (Marlborough)
.............................27 D4
Oxford Street (Swindon) 12 F3
P
Pack Hill........................20 G2
Packington Close 10 H2
Paddington Drive 11 C3
Paddock Close................5 C2
Paddock Lane 35 C2
Paddock, The (Highworth)
.............................31 C4
Paddocks House, The ..24 F1
Paddocks, The (Chippenham)
.............................24 F1
Paddocks, The
(Strat. St. Margaret) 7 C5
Page Close (Calne) 29 C3
Page Close (Chippenham)
.............................21 B6
Page Hay Cottages 1 D2
Paget Close 36 E3
Pagoda Park*, Mead Way
.............................11 A2
Pakenham Road 13 D5
Palmer Street................21 D6
Pans Lane 26 E5
Papermakers House*,
Rivenhall Road 11 A4
Parade Mews, The*,
Kennet Place 27 D4
Parade, The (Chippenham)
.............................21 D6
Parade, The (Marlborough)
.............................27 D4
Parade, The (Swindon) 37 A3
Paradise Path................31 C3
Parham Walk 10 F5
Parhams Court..............33 C3
Park Avenue (Chippenham)
.............................21 C5
Park Avenue (Highworth)
.............................31 C4
Park Close (Calne)........29 C4
Park Close (Malmesbury)
.............................32 F3
Park Dale Terrace 25 B4
Park Farm 5 C4
Park Gardens 30 E3
Park Lane (Chippenham)
.............................22 E5
Park Lane (Corsham)
........................35 C2/D1
Park Lane (Lydiard Millicent)
...............................9 D2
Park Lane (Malmesbury)
.............................32 E3
Park Lane (Swindon) 12 E3
Park Mead 32 F3
Park Road (Malmesbury)
.............................32 E2
Park Road (N. Tidworth)
.............................36 G4
Park Springs..................11 A4
Park Street 8 E5
Park Terrace 21 D5
Park View 25 B4
Park View Drive 9 D1
Park View Villas 29 A4
Park View*, Elcot Lane
.............................28 G4
Park Villas*, New Park Road
.............................26 E3
Parkfield (Devizes) 26 F2
Parkfields (Chippenham)
.............................21 D5
Parkfields Court 21 D5
Parklands (Chippenham)
.............................22 E4
Parklands (Malmesbury)
.............................32 E3
Parklands Road ..13 A4/37 D5
Parkside (Chippenham) 22 E5
Parkside (Swindon) 7 C4
Parkside*, The Hyde 3 D3
Parkstone Walk 13 D6
Parliament Row 32 G5
Parliament Street 21 C6
Parr Close 10 G3
Parrock, The..................27 D4
Parsley Close 5 B2
Parsonage Court 31 C3
Parsonage Farm Close..30 F4
Parsonage Road 7 C4
Parsonage Way 22 G3/G4
Parsons Way 33 B3
Partridge Close
(Chippenham) 21 C3
Partridge Close
(Corsham) 35 C3
Partridge Close
(Swindon) 14 G3
Passmore Close............14 G2
Pasture Close................11 C2
Patchway (Chippenham)
.............................21 C5
Patchway, The (Devizes)
.............................26 G4
Patford Street 29 B4
Patney Walk 6 F1
Patten Alley*, Oxford Street
.............................27 D4
Paul Street 35 C4
Paulet Close..................10 G5
Pauls Croft 30 G4
Pavely Close 23 D1
Paven Close 3 A3
Pavenhill..........................3 A3
Payne Close 24 F3
Peak, The 3 B4
Peaks Down 4 H5
Pearce Close 7 A1
Pearl Road 10 F2
Peartree Close 3 C2
Peat Moor........................5 A6
Peat Moor Way 4 G6
Peel Circus....................35 C2
Pelhams Court 28 E4
Pembroke Gardens 5 C4
Pembroke Road 24 H3
Pembroke Street 37 A6
Pen Close........................6 E3
Pencarrow Close 5 C1
Pendennis Road 10 G6
Penfold Gardens 12 G5
Penhill Drive 6 F2/G2
Penleigh Close 35 D4
Penn Hill Road 29 C3
Pennine Way 1 B6
Pennings Road..............36 E4
Penny Lane (Chippenham)
.............................24 G3
Penny Lane (Swindon) ..13 B2
Pennycress Close 5 C3
Penrose Walk................13 C4
Pentridge Close 14 E2
Pentylands Close 31 B2
Penzance Drive 11 C4
Pepperbox Hill 4 H5
Percheron Close 10 G2
Percy Jefferies Court 12 H1
Percy Street 11 D2
Peregrine Close 14 F1
Periwinkle Close..............5 A4
Perrys Lane 18 E5
Peshawar Close 36 E3
Peter Furkins Court*,
Wescott Place 12 E4
Petersfield Green..........36 G4
Petersfield Road............13 D5
Petter Close 18 F4
Pevensey Way 11 A4
Pew Hill..........................22 F4
Pew Hill House 22 F3
Pewsey House 36 G4
Pewsey Road 27 D5
Pewsham Lock 24 F2
Pewsham Road 6 H2
Pewsham Way 24 F2/G3
Pheasant Close
(Chippenham) 23 A1
Pheasant Close (Swindon)
.............................14 G3
Phelps Parade 29 B4
Phillip Close (Devizes) ..26 F3
Phillips Close (Cheltenham)
.............................21 A5
Phillips Place 12 H5
Phoenix Place*, Gains Lane
.............................26 E3
Phoenix Square 34 G5
Picketleaze....................21 B6
Pickford Way 6 E1
Pickwick Close 7 A2
Pickwick Road 35 B4
Picton Road 10 G2
Pictor Close 35 C2
Pigeon House Cottages ..8 G2
Pigeon House Lane 7 C4
Pike House Close..........30 E3
Pilgrim Close 10 G2
Pilton Close 10 F1
Pine Walk......................25 D5
Pinehurst Road................6 F6
Pines Road....................26 F5
Pinetree House*, Forest Dr.
.............................36 F6
Pinetree Rise 6 F4
Pinetum Close 25 D5
Pinfield Lane 24 G3
Pinhills 29 A5
Pinnacle, The*, Horder Mews
.............................12 H5
Pinnegar Way 14 G3
Pinnocks Place................7 B3
Pintail Court 34 G3
Pioneer Close................10 F2
Pipers Close..................33 A5
Pipers Piece..................27 D3
Pipers Way..............18 G2/H2
Pipitdene........................14 F2
Pippin Row*, The Pippin
.............................29 B4
Pippin, The 29 B4
Pipsmore Road..............21 B5
Pitchens Corner 18 F6
Pitchens, The 18 F6
Pittsfield 30 F4
Planks, The 12 H5
Plantation Road
(Chippenham) 21 D5
Plantation Road
(N. Tidworth) 36 H5
Plassey Road 36 F4
Plattes Close 10 H1
Play Close 3 C3
Plaza, The*, Sandford Street
.............................12 G3
Pleydell Road................18 G1
Pleydells 30 F3
Plume of Feathers Lane*,
London Road 28 E4
Plummer Close..............17 D5
Plumpton Close 23 A1
Plymouth Street 37 D3
Poachers Way 1 B6
Pockeridge Drive 35 D1
Pockeridge Road 35 D3
Police Houses*,
Five Stiles Road....28 F5
Poltondale......................14 F2
Pond Street 5 D2
Pons Close 28 F3
Ponting Street..........37 B2/C2
Pontings Close 2 E3
Pool Gastons Road 32 F3
Poole Road 5 C4
Poor Street 3 A4
Pope Close......................5 D2
Popham Court 24 F1
Poplar Avenue 6 G5
Poplars, The..................21 B4
Popplechurch Drive 14 G2
Port Hill..........................27 D1
Portal Close 21 D4
Portal Place 34 G3
Portal Road 6 E5
Porte Marsh Road 29 C2
Porth Close 4 H1
Portland Avenue............12 E5
Portland Way 29 C5
Portmore Close 5 A5
Portsmouth Street 37 D3
Portway 23 C1
Portwell..........................30 F4
Post Office Lane............35 B5
Potley Lane 35 D3
Potterdown Road 6 G1
Potterne Road 25 D6
Potters Walk..................33 A3
Poulton Cottages 28 E3
Poulton Crescent 28 E3
Poulton Farm Cottages 28 E3
Poulton Hill 28 E4
Poulton House Cottages
.............................28 F3
Poulton Street 12 G1
Pound Close..................34 F1
Pound Lane 6 F5
Pound Mead..................35 D4
Pound Pill......................35 C5
Pound Road 31 B2/B3
Powell Rise 32 H2
Poynder Road 35 B3
Poynings Way................10 F5
Preshute Lane 27 A5
Preston Lane 34 G2
Pretoria Villas*, Bath Road
.............................25 B4
Priestley Grove..............29 C5
Primrose Close (Calne) 29 B2
Primrose Close (Swindon)
...............................5 B2
Primrose Way................21 C3
Prince Charles Drive 29 C3
Prince Maurice Court 26 H1
Prince Rupert Court 10 G5
Princes Cottages 13 D6
Princes Court 36 E4
Princes Street................37 B3
Princess Gardens..........33 B3
Prior Park Cottages*,
Calcutt Street........30 G3
Priors Hill 18 F6
Priorsfield 28 E5
Priory Green..................31 C3
Priory Mews 32 H5
Priory New Road 35 A4
Priory Road 13 C5
Priory Street 35 A4
Priory, The (Cricklade) ..30 G2
Priory, The (Marlborough)
.............................27 D5
Pritchard Close................7 B2
Prospect........................35 C5
Prospect Hill 37 B5
Prospect Place (Swindon)
........................37 C5/C6
Prospect Place*, Blowhorn St.
.............................28 E4
Prospect West 21 B5
Proud Close 3 B4
Proudman Road............26 G3
Providence Lane 35 B4
Providence Terrace 22 E5
Provis Mead..................24 H3
Purbeck Close 14 E2
Purbeck Place 29 D5
Purcells Court................28 E5
Purleigh Road................35 B3
Purley Avenue 13 D6
Purley Close 18 F5
Purley Road 20 H2
Purlyn Acre....................27 D3
Purslane Close*,
Periwinkle Close 5 A4
Purton Court....................3 C3
Purton Road (Cricklade) 30 F5
Purton Road (Swindon)
................4 G5/H5/5 B4
Q
Quadrangle, The 23 D1
Quakers Walk................26 E2
Quarr Barton..................29 B4
Quarries, The (Swindon)
.............................12 G6
Quarry Close 26 G4
Quarry Crescent............31 B3
Quarry Mews 12 G6
Quarry Road..................37 B6
Quarry, The (Calne) 29 B5
Quarrybrook Close..........8 G2
Quarrydale Close 29 B5
Queen Elizabeth Drive
..........................5 A2/A3
Queen Street 37 A3
Queenborough 11 A5
Queens Avenue (Highworth)
.............................31 C3
Queens Avenue (Pewsey)
.............................35 A4
Queens Crescent..........23 B1
Queens Drive 13 A3
Queens Road (Devizes) 25 D5
Queens Road (Wootton B.)
.............................33 B3
Queens Square 24 F1
Queens Way..................28 F5
Queensbridge Cottages 23 B4
Queensfield 6 H2
Queensfield Court*, Parkfields
.............................22 E5
Queintin Road 12 H6
Quemerford 29 C6
Quemerford Farm Cottages
.............................29 D6
R
Rabley Cottages 28 G1
Rabley Wood View........28 E3
Radcot Close 4 G6
Radley Close 14 E2
Radnor Close 26 F5
Radnor Street................12 E4

Radstock Avenue 13 D3
Radway Road 7 B4
Raffin Lane 34 F6
Raggett Street 37 B5
Raglan Close 19 A1
Rainer Close 7 D4
Raleigh Avenue 13 B2
Ramleaze Drive 10 G2/G3
Ramsbury Avenue 6 F2
Ramsthorn Close 5 B3
Randall Court 35 B2
Randall Crescent 10 G1
Randolph Close 13 B4
Rannoch Close 4 H5
Ransome Close 10 H1
Ratcoombe Road 4 G5
Ravenglass Road 11 A3
Ravens Walk 15 A1/33 D3
Ravenscroft 14 E1
Rawlings Close 8 G3
Rawlingswell Lane 28 E4
Rawlins Road 34 F5
Rawston Close 14 E3
Ray Close (Swindon) 6 E3
Ray Close (Chippenham) 24 G2
Raybrook Crescent 11 C2
Rayfield Grove 12 F1
Read Street 12 E4
Reading Street 12 F3
Recreation Ground Cottages 28 E5
Rectory Lane 30 G3
Red Gables Close 3 A4
Red Lion Lane 30 G3
Redbridge Close 11 D5
Redcap Gardens 10 G2
Redcliffe Street 11 D3
Redhorn Gardens 26 E5
Redhouse Way 5 B1
Redland 21 C5
Redlands Close 31 C5
Redlands Court 31 B5
Redlynch Close 6 G2
Redman Road 29 C1
Redposts Drive 11 C5
Redruth Close 13 D4
Redwing Avenue 21 C3
Reed Close*, Oamaru Way 26 G4
Reeds 30 E3
Reeds Corner*, Reeds Grd. 28 F5
Reeds Farm Road 32 G3
Reeds Ground 28 F5
Reeves Close 14 E5
Reeves Road 26 G6
Regent Circus 37 B4
Regent Close 37 B4
Regent House 37 B4
Regent Street 37 B4
Reids Piece 3 B4
Rendells Court 26 E4
Renoir Close 1 C5
Restrop Road 3 A5
Restrop View 3 A3
Retingham Way 7 C2
Retreat, The 31 B3
Revell Close 7 A3
Reynolds Way 1 C5
Rhine Close 11 D5
Rhuddlan 11 A5
Ricardo Road 22 E5
Richards Close 33 A4
Richmond Close 26 H1
Richmond Road (Calne) 29 A2
Richmond Road (Swindon) 6 E6
Rider Close 26 H1
Ridge Green 10 H2
Ridge Nether Moor 20 G1
Ridge, The 1 D3
Ridgemead 29 B2
Ridgeway Close 5 D5
Ridgeway House*, The Lawns 33 A3
Ridgeway Road 7 A2
Ridgeway, The 19 B6
Riding School Yard 27 D4
Ridings Mead 21 D3
Ridings, The*, Scarborough Rd. 11 D1
Ringsbury Close 3 A4
Ringwood Close 13 D3
Rinsdale Close 4 H6
Ripley Road 12 G5
Ripon Close 23 B2
Ripon Way 13 C6
Ripple Field 10 H5
Risingham Mead 11 A4
Rivenhall Road 11 A4
River Park 27 D5
River Street (Chippenham) 22 E6
River Street (Pewsey) 34 G5
River View (Chippenham) 22 E6
River View (Malmesbury) 32 F3/H4
Riverdale Close 18 G1
Riverdale Walk 18 G1
Riverhouse*, St. Mary Street 22 F6
Rivermead Drive 11 A1/A2
Rivers Way 31 B3
Riverside Drive 22 G6
Riverside*, Stockley La. 29 C6
Roberts Close 18 F6
Robinia Close 34 G4
Robins Close (Chippenham) 21 C3
Robins Close (Wootton B.) 15 A1/33 D3
Robinsgreen 14 F2
Robinson Close 14 F3
Rochdale Avenue 29 B2
Roche Close 14 F5
Rochester Close 10 H5
Rochford Close 10 G4
Rockdown Court 6 H3
Rodbourne Road 11 D2/12 E3
Rodwell Close 13 C5
Roebuck Close 33 C4
Roebuck Meadow 28 F4
Rogers Close 13 C2
Rogers Meadow 27 D2
Rolleston Street 37 B5
Roman Court (Blunsdon) 1 D3
Roman Court (Pewsey) 34 F5
Roman Crescent 12 F6
Roman Way (Chippenham) 24 H2
Roman Way (Highworth) 31 B4
Romney Way 10 G3
Romsey Street 11 D2
Ron Golding Close 32 G2
Rooks Nest Close 24 G3
Rope Yard 33 A4
Rosary, The 33 B3
Rose Street 11 D2
Rosebery Street 37 C2
Rosedale Road 13 D5
Roseland Avenue 26 F4
Rosemary Close 5 B2
Rosewood Court (Swindon) 14 F6
Rosewood Court*, Forest Dr. 36 F6
Ross Gardens 7 C3
Rother Close 5 D2
Rotherstone 25 D3
Roughmoor Farm Close 4 F6
Roughmoor Way 10 G1/G2
Round House 29 D6
Roundhills Mead 31 C1/C4
Roundway Down 10 H6
Roundway Gardens 26 E1
Roundway Park 26 F1/F2
Rowan Close*, Broomcroft Road 34 G4
Rowan Cottages 35 A3
Rowan Court*, Chestnut Av. 36 E5
Rowan Drive 33 C4
Rowan Road 6 E4
Rowans, The 32 F3
Rowdefield Farm Cottages 25 C1
Rowden Hill 23 D1
Rowden Lane 23 D2
Rowden Place 23 C2
Rowden Road 23 D1
Rowe Mead 24 F2
Rowland Hill Close 14 G5
Rowton Heath Way 10 G4/G5
Royal Close 24 E1
Royal Crescent, The 36 F5
Royal Oak Close 24 G1
Royal Oak Court*, Commercial Rd. 26 E3
Royal Oak Road*, Commercial Rd. 26 E3
Royston Road 13 C5
Rubens Close 1 B5
Ruckley Gardens 7 D5
Rumble Dene 24 F2
Rupert Close 26 H1
Rural Gardens*, London Rd. 24 F1
Rushall Close 6 F2
Rushmere Path*, Westfield Way 5 D2
Rushton Road 13 C6
Ruskin Avenue 7 B3/B4
Ruskin Drive 33 C2
Russell Square 27 D4
Russell Walk 13 A3
Russells Yard*, High Street 27 D5
Russley Close 4 F6
Rutland Road 13 B4
Ruxley Close 33 A5
Ryan Avenue 21 B6
Ryan Close 4 H5
Rycote Close 10 G3
Rydal Close 5 D2
Rye Close 10 G2
Rylands Way 33 B3
S
Sackville Close 13 B2
Saddle Back Close 29 C5
Saddleback Road 10 G2
Sadler Walk 13 B4
Sadlers Mead 22 F5/G6
Saffron Close (Swindon) 5 B4
Saffron Close (Wootton B.) 33 B1
Sage Close 5 B2
Salamander Court 36 F5
Salcombe Grove 13 B4
Salisbury Close 23 A1
Salisbury Hill 28 E6
Salisbury House 36 F4
Salisbury Road (Marlborough) 28 E5
Salisbury Road (N. Tidworth) 36 H4
Salisbury Road (Pewsey) 34 F6
Salisbury Street (Devizes) 25 B4
Salisbury Street (Swindon) 37 C2
Salmons Leap 29 A1
Saltersford Lane 23 B2
Saltram Close 14 E3
Salzgitter Court 11 A4
Salzgitter Drive 1 C5/D6
Sams Lane 2 E3
Sandacre Road 10 F1/G1
Sandalwood Court 7 D3
Sandes Close 21 D6
Sandford Court 12 G6
Sandford House*, Croft Road 12 G6
Sandgate 7 D6
Sandgate Mews 7 D6
Sandown Avenue 13 A6
Sandown Drive 23 A2
Sandpiper Bridge 14 G2
Sandpiper Gardens 21 C3
Sandpit Road 29 C2
Sandringham Road 13 B6
Sandstone Road 1 B6
Sandwood Close 4 H5
Sandy Lane 12 F5
Sandy Ridge 29 C5
Sanford Street 37 B3
Sarsen Close 11 D5
Sarsen Court 26 H1
Sarum Drive 26 E5
Sarum Road 23 B1
Sarum Way 29 A4
Sassoon Walk 27 B4
Saunders Grove 35 C2
Savernake Court 28 E5
Savernake Crescent 28 F5
Savernake Drive 29 A4
Savernake House*, Ordnance Road 36 G4
Savernake Road 35 D2
Savernake Street 37 A5
Savill Crescent 17 D4
Sawyer Road 6 F1
Saxby Road 22 F4
Saxon Close 30 F4
Saxon Court (N. Tidworth) 36 F4
Saxon Court (Swindon) 12 H5
Saxon Mill 19 B5
Saxon Street 21 C5
Saxton Walk 10 H1
Scarborough Road 11 D1
Scarlet Close 1 B6
School Close (Strat. St. Margaret) 7 C4
School Close (Chiseldon) 19 B5
School Court 6 H6
School House Court*, Shrivenham Road 31 C5
School Lane (Marlborough) 27 A5
School Lane (Wroughton) 18 E5
School Road 29 A2
School Row 5 C3
School View 34 E5
School Walk 21 B6
Scotby Avenue 13 A6
Scotchel Green 34 G4
Scotney Crescent 5 D1
Scotton Place*, New Park St. 25 D3
Seagry Court 6 F2
Seaton Close 5 D2
Sedgebrook 20 F1
Sedgefield Gardens 26 E3
Sedgefield Way 23 A1
Sefton Road 4 H1
Selby Crescent 10 H5
Seldon Close 13 A3
Selions Close 21 C3
Semley Walk 6 G3
Sevenfields 31 C2
Severn Avenue 5 D3
Severn Close 29 A2
Sewage Farm Cottages*, Barnfield Close 11 D2
Seymour Road (Chippenham) 22 G5
Seymour Road (Swindon) 13 B3
Shackelton Road 26 G5
Shaftesbury Avenue 13 D6
Shaftesbury Close 3 C2
Shakespeare Drive 27 C5
Shakespeare Path 7 B4
Shakespeare Road 33 C2
Shalbourne Close*, Downton Road 6 F2
Shambles, The*, Tetbury Hill 32 G3
Shanklin Road 5 C3
Shaplands 7 C5
Shapwick Close 14 E2
Sharp Close 10 H2
Shaw Road 11 A3
Shearwood Road 4 G6
Sheen Close 10 F5
Sheep Street (Devizes) 26 E4
Sheep Street (Highworth) 31 C3
Sheeps Croft 21 C3
Sheerwold Close 7 D3
Sheffield Lane 35 C2
Shelburne Road 29 C5
Shelburne Terrace 29 C5
Sheld Drive 34 G2
Sheldon Road 21 C6
Shelfinch 11 B5
Shelley Avenue 33 D2
Shelley Street 12 F4
Shenton Close 7 D4
Shenton Court 7 D4
Shepherds Breech 33 B3
Sheppard Close (Chippenham) 24 G2
Sheppard Close (Devizes) 25 D3
Sheppard Street 37 A2
Shepperton Way 5 D1/6 E1
Sherborne Place*, Tyneham Road 13 D3
Sherfields 33 C4
Sherford Road 5 C3
Sheridan Drive 33 C2
Sheringham Court*, Liden Dr. 14 F6
Sherington Mead 24 H3
Sherston Avenue 6 G2
Sherston Road 32 E3
Sherwood Road 13 D5
Shetland Close 10 G2
Shipley Drive 5 D1
Shipton Grove 13 A4
Shipton Hill*, Gloucester Rd. 32 G3
Shire Close 10 G2
Shire Court 12 E4
Shirley Close 13 B2
Showell Cottages 23 C4
Showfield 33 B2
Shrewsbury Road 13 B3
Shrewton Walk 6 G1
Shrivenham Road (Highworth) 31 C5
Shrivenham Road (Swindon) 37 D3
Shropshire Close 10 H2
Sidbury Circular Road 36 E3
Sidbury Hill Avenue 36 E4
Sidings, The 25 C4
Sidmouth Parade*, Sidmouth Street 26 E4
Sidmouth Street 26 E4
Sidney Close (Grange Park) 10 F5

Sidney Close (Swindon) 13 A3
Sidney Wood Court 21 D6
Sigerson Road 5 A2
Signal Way 12 H6
Silbury Close 23 B2
Silbury Mews 5 C4
Silbury Road 29 A4
Silchester Way 11 A3
Silman Close 35 B2
Silto Court 5 D6
Silver Street (Calne) 29 B6
Silver Street (Malmesbury) 32 G4
Silverless Street 27 D4
Silverton Road 13 D3
Silveston Way 32 E3
Simnel Close 10 F4
Skeete Court 13 D5
Skew Bridge Close 33 A5
Skye Close 31 B2
Slade Drive 13 C1/D1
Slade House*, Sedgefield Gdns. 26 E3
Slades, The 29 C3
Slater Road 34 F5
Slaters Orchard*, Ermin St. 7 C4
Sleaford Close 10 G3
Sleight Road 26 H6
Slessor Road 34 G3
Slipper Lane 19 A6
Smitan Brook 14 F3
Smiths Yard 35 B5
Snails Lane 25 D4
Snapps Close 18 F6
Snowdon Place 7 A3
Snowdrop Close*, Cornflower Road 5 B2
Snowshill Close 5 D2
Snuff Court 25 D3
Snuff Street 25 D3
Somerdale Close 11 A3
Somerford Close 6 H3
Somerset Road 5 D6
Somerville Road 13 B3
Sorley Close 27 B5
Sorrel Close 33 B1
Sorrel Drive 21 C2
Sound Copse 4 H5
South Avenue 35 B5
South Drive*, Blunsdon Abbey Caravan Pk. 1 B5
South Leaze Cottages 11 B6
South Place (Calne) 29 B5
South Place (Corsham) 35 C5
South Street (Corsham) 35 C5
South Street (Swindon) 37 B6
South View (Wootton B.) 33 C2
South View Avenue 13 A4
South View Cottages (Wanborough) 14 H5
South View Court 26 E5
South View Place 28 E4
South View*, Bremilham Rd. 32 F4
Southampton Street 37 D4
Southbank Glen 33 C3
Southbrook Street 12 F1
Southbroom Road 26 E4
Southcott Road 34 G6
Southern View 28 G3
Southernwood Drive 5 A3
Southerwicks 35 C4
Southey Close 1 B5
Southfield*, Hodson Rd. 19 D6
Southgate 26 E5
Southgate Close 26 E5
Southmead 21 C6
Southmead Road 23 C1
Southview Cottages (S. Marston) 8 G4
Southwell Close 23 B2
Southwick Avenue 6 F2
Southwold Close 4 H1
Spa Close 31 D2/D3
Spackman Lane 35 C3
Spanbourn Avenue 22 E5
Sparcells Drive 4 H5
Sparrow Lane 33 A3
Speedwell Close*, Cloudberry Road 5 C2
Speer Court 26 E6
Spencer Close 10 F2
Spencers Orchard 18 E5
Spenser Close 13 C2
Speresholt 11 B5
Spindle Tree Court 6 F5
Spinney Close 23 B1
Spital Lane 30 G4
Spitfire Way 8 E1
Spode Close 1 A6
Sprats Barn Crescent 33 A3
Spring Close 37 B3
Spring Gardens 37 C3
Spring Lane (Calne) 29 B5
Spring Lane (Corsham) 35 D1
Springers Close 26 G3
Springfield Buildings 22 E5
Springfield Crescent 33 A2
Springfield Drive 29 A3
Springfield House*, The Lawns 33 A3
Springfield Road (Devizes) 25 A1
Springfield Road (Swindon) 12 G6
Springhill Close 11 A4
Spruce Court 6 F5
Spur Way 7 A4
Square, The (Calne) 29 B4
Square, The (Pewsey) 34 F5
Square, The (Swindon) 12 H5
Squires Copse 4 G6
Squires Hill Close 33 D3
Squirrel Crescent 33 C3
St. Albans Close 11 C2
St. Aldhelm Road 32 F3
St. Aldhelms Close 32 F3
St. Ambrose Close 14 F3
St. Andrews Close 18 F4
St. Andrews Court (Blunsden) 1 A5
St. Andrews Court (Wroughton) 18 F4
St. Andrews Green 14 G2
St. Andrews Road 36 F4
St. Austell Way 11 D3
St. Barbaras Road 35 D2
St. Bridget Close 26 G4
St. Catherines Close 29 C3
St. Clements Court (Chippenham) 21 D5
St. Clements Court (Swindon) 13 C5
St. Davids Way 27 D4
St. Dennis Road 32 G4
St. Dunstan Close 29 B2
St. Francis Avenue 23 D1
St. Georges Close 36 G4
St. Georges Road 36 G4
St. Helens View 11 D5
St. Ives Court 13 D2
St. James Close 6 H2
St. James Gardens 26 E3
St. James Place*, Southbroom Rd. 26 E4
St. John Road 18 E5
St. Johns Close (Marlborough) 27 D3
St. Johns Close (Pewsey) 34 H5
St. Johns Court 25 D4
St. Johns Street (Devizes) 25 D4
St. Johns Street (Malmesbury) 32 H5
St. Josephs Drive 23 D1
St. Josephs Place 25 C3
St. Katherine Green 14 F2
St. Lukes Court 27 C3
St. Lukes Drive 23 D1
St. Margarets Close 29 A3
St. Margarets Cottages*, Culvermead Cl. 28 E5
St. Margarets Gardens 23 D1
St. Margarets Green 7 D5
St. Margarets Mead 28 F5
St. Margarets Road 12 H6
St. Martins 28 E4
St. Mary Street (Chippenham) 22 F6
St. Marys Cottages*, Commercial Rd. 26 E3
St. Marys Courtyard*, Church Street 29 B4
St. Marys Gardens 26 E3
St. Marys Grove 12 F1
St. Marys Lane*, Gloucester Road 32 G4
St. Marys Place 22 E5
St. Marys Street (Malmesbury) 32 G3
St. Mellion Close 22 G6
St. Michaels Avenue (Highworth) 31 A3/B3
St. Michaels Avenue (N. Tidworth) 36 H4
St. Michaels Court*, Oxford Street 32 G4
St. Michaels Green 36 G4
St. Michaels View 36 F5
St. Nicholas Close 29 C3
St. Patricks Avenue 36 G3
St. Paul Street 22 E5
St. Pauls Drive 14 F2/G2
St. Pauls Street 6 G6
St. Peters Close 23 D1
St. Philips Road 7 A3
St. Teresas Drive 21 D6
Stables Court (Marlborough) 27 D4
Stable Court (Wootton B.) 33 A3
Stables, The*, Academy Dr. 35 B3
Stafford Street 37 A5
Stainers Way 21 B3/C2
Stamford Close 10 H4
Stanbridge Park 10 G2
Stanbrook Close 27 A6
Stancombe Park 11 B4
Standen Way 1 C6
Standings Close 10 G1
Stanford Court 26 E4
Stanier Road 29 C1
Stanier Street 37 A5
Stanley Honey Court 13 B3
Stanley Lane 24 H2
Stanley Street 37 C5
Stanley Terrace 26 E5
Stanley Villas 26 E5
Stanmore Street 12 E4
Stansfield Close 11 A5
Stanway Close 13 C5
Stapleford Close 24 F3
Stapleford Way 6 F1
Stapleton Close 31 B3
Staring Close 10 F1
Station Approach*, Newport Street 12 H6
Station Hill 22 E5
Station Road (Calne) 29 B5
Station Road (Chiseldon) 19 B5
Station Road (Corsham) 35 C5
Station Road (Devizes) 25 D3
Station Road (Highworth) 31 B3
Station Road (N. Tidworth) 36 G4
Station Road (Purton) 3 C3
Station Road (Swindon) 37 A2
Station Road (Wootton B.) 33 A4
Station View 33 B5
Station Yard 3 C2
Staverton Way*, Westwood Road 6 G1
Steadings, The 33 C4
Stedham Walk*, Priory Road 13 D5
Steele Close 26 G3
Stenbury Close 1 C6
Stenness Close 5 A5
Stephens Road 13 C1
Stephenson Road 2 E6
Stevenson Road 5 A2
Stewart Close (Chippenham) 24 G3
Stewart Close (Swindon) 6 F1
Stirling Close 18 E4
Stirling Road 8 E1
Stockbridge Copse 4 H5
Stockham Close 30 G3
Stockley Lane 29 D6
Stocks Close 20 H6
Stockton Road 6 G3
Stockwell Road 26 F3
Stockwood Road 23 C1
Stokes Close 26 H1
Stokes Croft 29 B3
Stokes Road 35 C5
Stokesay Drive 11 A4
Stone Grove 13 B5
Stone Lane 3 D6
Stonebridge Close 28 E4
Stonebridge Lane 28 E4
Stonecrop Way 5 C2
Stonefield Close 11 A2
Stonefield Drive 31 C4
Stonehill Green 11 B3
Stonehurst Close 13 C1
Stoneking Court 28 E5
Stonelea Close 21 C6
Stoneover Lane 33 C3
Stones Lane 30 E3
Stonybeck Close 11 B3
Stour Walk 6 F3
Strand, The 29 B4
Stranks Close 31 C5
Stratford Close 11 B4
Stratton Court 3 B3
Stratton Orchard 7 C5
Stratton Road (Pewsey) 34 F5
Stratton Road (Swindon) 13 B1
Stratton St. Margaret Bypass 7 A1/14 F1
Street, The (Lydiard Millicent) 9 C1
Street, The (Swindon) 5 C4
Stroma Way 31 A2
Strouds Hill 19 A5
Stuart Close 13 B3
Stubsmead 14 E4
Studland Close 13 D6
Sudeley Way 10 F4
Suffolk Street 12 G1
Summerhouse Road 17 D4
Summers Street 11 D2
Sumsions Drive 35 B2
Sun Lane 18 E6
Sunningdale Close 22 G6
Sunningdale Road 6 F3
Sunnyside Avenue 12 E5
Surrey Road 6 E6
Sussex Square 13 B3
Sussex Wharf 25 C3
Sutherland Crescent 21 C2
Sutton Park 2 E4
Sutton Place 26 E4
Sutton Road 14 E5
Swaddon Street 29 B3
Swallow Close 36 G5
Swallowdale 14 F2
Swallowfield Avenue 13 B4
Swallows Mead 15 A1/33 D3
Swan Cottages*, Green Drove 34 G6
Swan Meadow 34 G6
Swan Road (Corsham) 35 B2
Swan Road (Pewsey) 34 F6
Swanage Walk 5 C4
Swanborough Close 24 G3
Swanbrook 14 F1
Swayne Close 24 G2
Swift Avenue 1 C6
Swinburne Place 33 C2
Swindon House 36 F5
Swindon Road (Cricklade) 30 H4
Swindon Road (Highworth) 31 B6
Swindon Road (Malmesbury) 32 H5
Swindon Road (Strat. St. Margaret) 7 C4/C6
Swindon Road (Swindon) 37 B5
Swindon Road (Wootton B.) 15 B1/33 C1
Swindon Road (Wroughton) 18 F4
Swindon Street 31 C4
Swinley Drive 4 G6
Sword Gardens 11 D5
Sycamore Close (Lyneham) 34 H2
Sycamore Close (N. Tidworth) 36 F6
Sycamore Grove 6 G5
Symonds 10 H6
Syon Close (Corsham) 35 C3
Syon Close (Swindon) 5 D1
Sywell Road 14 E1
T
Tadpole Lane 1 A5
Tall Trees 22 E6
Tallis Walk 10 G4
Tamar Close 6 E3
Tamarisk Close 29 B5
Tamworth Drive 10 G2
Tanner Close 24 G2
Tanners Close 33 A3/A4
Tansley Moor 14 G6
Taplow Walk 13 C5
Tarka Close 1 B6
Tarragon Close 5 A3
Tasker Close 35 C3
Tatley Walk 20 G6
Tattershall 11 A6
Taunton Close 23 A2
Taunton Street 12 E3
Tavinor Drive 24 F3
Tavistock Road 13 D3
Tawny Owl Close 14 E1
Taylor Crescent 7 C3
Teal Avenue 34 G2
Tealsbrook 14 F2
Teasel Close 26 H5
Tedder Close 6 F5
Tees Close 6 E3
Teeswater Close 10 G3
Telford Way 11 B5
Tellcroft Close 35 D4
Templars Firs 33 B5
Temple Street 37 B4

Tenby Close 13 B6
Tennyson Close 27 B5
Tennyson Road 33 C2
Tennyson Street 12 F4
Tenzing Gardens 6 G4
Tern Close 29 D4
Terncliff 14 F2
Tetbury Hill 32 F1
Tewkesbury Way 10 E2/H4/11 A4
Thackeray Close 14 F5
Thames Avenue 5 C2/D2
Thames Close 30 G3
Thames Lane 30 G3
Thamesdown Drive 1 A6/B6/4 H1/5 A1
Thamesmead Cottages*, Thames Lane 30 G3
Thatcham Close 29 A2
Thatchers, The 2 E6
The Fairway 25 D6
Theatre Square 37 B4
Theobald Street 12 F3
Thetford Way 5 A2
Thirlmere 14 G6
Thirsk Close 23 B2
Thomas Court 29 C5
Thomas Mead 24 F2
Thomas Street 11 D2
Thomas Wyatt Road 26 E6
Thomson Way 27 B5
Thorley Close 6 E1
Thornbridge Avenue 13 C5
Thorne Road 14 E5
Thornford Drive 11 A4
Thornhill Cottages 32 E5
Thornhill Drive 1 B5
Thornhill Road 8 F5
Thorns, The 27 D2
Thresher Drive 6 G1
Thrushel Close 5 C3
Thurlestone Road 13 A4
Thurney Drive 10 F5
Thurnham Court*, Thomas Wyatt Rd. 26 E6
Thurston Court 22 E5
Thyme Close 5 A4
Tidworth Close 11 D5
Tilley Close 26 G3
Tilleys Lane 7 C6
Tilshead Walk 6 F2
Timandra Close 6 E1
Timber Street 22 F6
Timbrells Place 23 D1
Tin Pit 28 E3
Tinings, The 22 G5
Tinkers Field 33 B3
Tinkers Mead 34 G6
Tintagel Close 10 H5
Tintern Road 26 E6
Tisbury Close 6 G1
Tismeads Crescent 18 G1
Titchfield Close 10 F4
Tithe Barn Crescent 11 D5
Tiverton Road 6 G6
Tockenham Way*, Ramsbury Avenue 6 F1
Tollard Close 14 E3
Toothill Cottages 10 H5
Toppers Close 6 E4
Tornio Close 26 G2
Torr Close 21 C3
Torridge Close 5 D3
Torrington Court*, Welcombe Av. 13 C4
Totterdown Close 14 G2
Tovey Road 6 E5
Towcester Close*, Beverley Way 23 A2
Towcester Road 14 E1
Tower Road 4 H5
Town Mill 28 E4
Townsend Place 21 A5
Tracy Close 6 E1
Trafalgar Place 25 C3
Trajan Road 8 E6
Tregantle Walk 14 E3
Tregenna Villas*, Bath Road 25 B4
Tregoze Way 10 F3
Trenchard Close 23 B1
Trenchard Road 34 G3
Trent Road 6 E3
Trentham Close 13 C5
Triangle, The*, Bristol Street 32 G4
Tricentre Precinct 37 B3
Trinity Close 13 C6
Trinity House*, St. Georges Rd. 36 F4
Trinity Park 29 C6
Tropnell Close 35 C3
Trout Lane 35 D1
Trowbridge House 36 F4
Truman Close 14 E5
Truro Path 10 H5
Truro Walk 23 A1
Tryon Close 20 F1
Tudor Crescent 7 D6
Tudor Walk 13 B3
Tugela Road 22 F4
Tulip Tree Close 6 G5
Tupman Road 35 B3
Turl Street 37 B3
Turnball 19 A6
Turnberry Close 22 G6
Turner Street 12 E4
Turnham Green 10 G5
Turnpike (Swindon) 2 E6
Turnpike Road (Highworth) 31 C3
Turnpike Road (Swindon) 2 E5
Turnpike, The (Chippenham) 24 H2
Turpin Way 21 A6
Tweed Close 5 D3
Twickenham Way 22 F4
Twyford Close 13 C3
Twynnoy Close 32 H2
Tyburn Close 10 H4
Tydeman Street 6 H6
Tye Gardens 10 F4
Tylees Court*, Sutton Place 26 E4
Tyndale Path 10 G4
Tyneham Road 13 D3
Tyning Park 29 C6
Tynings, The 35 C4
U
Ullswater Close 14 G6
Union Road 22 E5
Union Row 37 C6
Union Street 37 C5
Unity Street 21 D6
Upavon Court 6 G2
Upfield 14 F6
Upham Road 37 D5
Upham Road Centre, The 37 D5
Upper Churchfields 28 E6
Upper Isbury 28 E5
Upper Pavenhill 3 A3
Upper Widhill Lane 1 B3/C4
Upton Close 5 D2
Urchfont House 36 F5
Urchfont Way 6 G3
Utah Close 11 D5
Utterson View 21 D6
Uxbridge Road 10 G6
V
Vale Court 30 F3
Vale Road 34 E5
Vale View 33 A4
Valley Road 35 B3
Valley View 32 H6
Valley Way 29 A5
Valleyside 12 E5
Van Diemens Close 28 E5
Vanbrugh Gate 19 B2
Vasterne Close 3 B3
Ventnor Close 5 C3
Verney Close 14 F3
Verulam Close 14 F1
Verwood Close 13 C4
Vespasian Close 14 E1
Vicarage Close (Calne) 29 C4
Vicarage Close (Marlborough) 28 E4
Vicarage Gardens 32 H5
Vicarage Lane 31 C3
Vicarage Road 5 D6
Victoria Cross Road 17 D4
Victoria Drive 34 H2
Victoria Road (Devizes) 26 E3
Victoria Road (Swindon) 37 C4
Victoria Terrace 29 B3
Victory Row 33 A3
View Close 32 F3
Viking Close 1 B6
Villiers Close (Chipppenham) 22 G6
Villiers Close (Swindon) 10 F2
Vincients Road 21 A5
Viscount Way 8 E1
Vockins Close 36 E4
Volpe Close 10 F5
Volta Road 37 B3
Vorda Road 31 C2
Vowley View 33 C4
W
Waggon Yard*, London Road 28 E4
Waggoner Close 6 F1
Wagtail Close 14 E1
Waiblingen Way 25 D3
Wainwright Close 14 F5
Waite Meads Close 3 C3
Wakefield Close 10 G5
Walcot Road 37 D4
Walden Lodge Close 26 E5
Waldron Close 14 E5
Walker House 6 E4
Wallingford Close 11 A5
Wallis Drive 1 C5
Wallsworth Road 13 C5
Walnut Close 34 G5
Walnut Court 7 A5
Walnut Tree Close 7 D4
Walnut Tree Gardens 9 D1
Walnuts, The 3 D6
Walsingham Road 13 B3
Walter Close 10 G3
Walter Sutton Close*, Long Barrow Rd. 29 A4
Walton Close 13 B4
Walwayne Field 7 C2
Wanborough Road 8 E6/14 G2
Wansdyke Drive 29 A4
Wanshot Close 18 G6
Warbeck Gate 10 F4
Wardley Close 13 C5
Wardour Close 13 A6
Wardour Road 23 B1
Wareham Close 10 H4
Warminster Avenue 6 G2
Warminster House*, Wylye Road 36 F5
Warneford Close 11 B5
Warner Close 7 D4
Warren Crescent 29 C2
Warrener Close 1 D6
Warwick Close 23 A2
Warwick Road 37 B5
Washbourne Road 33 B4
Wastfield 35 D4
Water Field 3 A4
Water Furlongs 30 F4
Watercrook Mews 11 A4
Waterdown Close 5 A3
Watermead 8 E5
Watermeadows 32 G5
Waters Edge 24 F2
Waterside Park 26 H1
Waterside Way 20 F2
Watling Close 11 C3
Wavell Road (N. Tidworth) 36 E3
Wavell Road (Swindon) 6 F5
Waverley Court 35 C4
Waverley Road 8 E6
Waylands (Cricklade) 30 G4
Waylands (Devizes) 26 G4
Wayne Close 6 E2
Ways Way 34 F4
Wayside Close 11 C2
Weavern Court*, Frogwell 21 B6
Weavers Close (Chippenham) 21 A6
Weavers Close (Malmesbury) 32 G2
Weavers House*, The Green 29 B4
Weavers, The 12 H5
Webb Close 24 F2
Webbington Road 24 F2
Webbs Court 34 F1
Webbs Lane 25 C4
Webbs Way 32 G3
Webbs Wood 4 G5
Wedgewood Close 12 E2
Wedmore Avenue 21 D4
Weedon Road 13 C1
Weirside Avenue 18 F5
Welbeck Close 13 B4
Welcombe Avenue 13 C4
Welford Close 14 E1
Weller Road 35 B4
Wellington Drive*, Horton Rd. 26 H1
Wellington Mews 37 A2
Wellington Place 27 D5
Wellington Road 36 E6
Wellington Street 37 A2
Well Close (Chiseldon) 19 A6
Wells Close (Chippenham) 23 B2
Wells Street 37 C4
Welton Road 11 B3
Wembley Street 11 D1
Wenhill Cottages 29 A5
Wenhill Heights 29 B5
Wenhill Lane 29 A5
Wensleydale Close 10 H2
Wentworth Close 22 G6
Wentworth Park 10 G5
Were, The*, Dixon Way 29 B3
Wesley Court 33 C2
Wesley Street 37 C6
Wessex Close (Calne) 29 C3
Wessex Close*, Cornfield Rd. 26 G4
Wessex Road 21 C5
Wessex Way 31 D2
Wessington Avenue 29 C6
Wessington Court 29 C6/C5
West Cepen Way 21 A5/B3/23 A1/A3
West Drive (Marlborough) 27 D5
West Drive*, Blunsdon Abbey Caravan Park 1 B5
West End Road 7 C6
West Highland Road 1 B6
West Hill 1 D3
West Leaze Cottages 17 D1
West Manton 27 A6
West Mill Lane 30 E3
West Park Road 35 B3
West Street 32 F4
West View 13 D2
West View Cresent 25 C4
Westbourne Court 11 D3
Westbrook Close 21 B6
Westbrook Road 6 E6
Westbury House*, Nadder Road 36 G5
Westbury Park 33 A5
Westbury Road 6 F2
Westcott Place 12 E4
Westcott Street 12 E4
Westcroft 23 B2
Westerham Walk 29 C5
Westerleigh Close 23 C1
Western Street 37 B5
Westfield Way 5 B3/C2
Westhill Close 31 B4
Westlea Drive 11 A4
Westlecot Road 12 F6
Westlecott Farm Cottages 18 F1
Westmead Drive 11 B3
Westmead Lane 22 E6
Westmead Terrace 24 F1
Westminster Gardens 21 C6
Westminster Road 10 H5/11 A5
Westmorland Road 37 D4
Westridge 25 D3
Westrop 31 B3
Westwood Road 6 G1
Wetherby Close 23 A2
Wey Close 6 E3
Weyhill Close 13 C4
Whalley Crescent 17 D5
Wharf Road 16 G2/17 A2/C3
Wharf Street 25 D3
Wharf, The*, Couch Lane 25 D3
Wharf, The*, Patford Street 29 B4
Wheatlands 5 C3
Wheatstone Road 14 G5
Wheeler Avenue 6 H4/7 A5
Wheeler Close 34 E4
Whilestone Way 8 E6
Whistley Road 25 A5/A6
Whitbourne Avenue 13 B4
Whitbourne House 13 C4
Whitbred Close 10 H2
Whitby Grove 5 D6
White Beam Court 6 F5
White Castle 11 A6
White Edge Moor 14 G6/20 F1
White Horse Road 30 F3
White Horse Way 29 B5
White Lion Park 32 E3
White Road 28 H6
Whitefield Crescent 4 G6
Whitehall Cottages 30 E6
Whitehall Gardens*, Quarr Barton 29 B4
Whitehead Street 12 F4
Whitehill Lane 33 A4
Whitehill Way 10 F5
Whitehorn Close 33 B1
Whitehouse Road 12 F1/G2
Whitelands Road 7 C6
Whiteman Street 12 G1
Whitgift Close 10 F3
Whitmore Close 10 F3
Whitney Street 37 B4
Whittington Road 11 A3
Whittle Close 21 B6
Whitworth Road (Chippenham) 24 F2
Whitworth Road (Swindon) 6 E4

Wichelstok Close 12 G6
Wick Close 7 A2
Wick Lane (Devizes) ...26 E5
Wick Lane (Swindon) ...20 G1
Wick Lane (Wanborough)
..................................14 H3
Wickdown Avenue 5 D4
Wickfield 26 E5
Wicks Close 5 C2
Wicks Drive 24 G2
Widhill Cottages 1 B2
Wigmore Avenue 13 B5
Wilcot Avenue 6 H2
Wilcot Road 34 E4
Wilcox Close 6 G5
Wildern Square 7 C3
Wilderness Row*,
   Easterton Lane ..34 G6
Wilkins Close 7 B2
William Road 26 G5
William Robbins Court*,
   Moredon Road 5 C4
William Street (Calne) .29 C2
William Street (Swindon)
..................................12 E4
William Stumpes Close..32 F2
Williams Grove 35 C5
Willis Close 24 G3
Willis Court 26 E3
Willis Way 3 B4
Willow Close 28 G4
Willow Drive 26 H2
Willow Grove 22 F3
Willow House Flats*,
   Downlands Road ..26 E6
Willow Mews*, Forest Drive
..................................36 F6
Willow View Close 32 F3
Willow Walk 18 F5
Willowbank 21 B3
Willowbrook 3 C3
Willowherb Close 5 C2
Willows Avenue 6 G4
Willows, The (Highworth)
..................................31 C4
Willows, The (Swindon) ..4 G5
Willows, The*, Park Rd. 32 F3
Willows, The*, Tebury Hill
..................................32 G3
Wills Avenue................13 A1
Wilmot Close 10 F3
Wilson House*,
   Sidbury Circ. Rd. ..36 E4
Wilson Road 5 D1
Wilton Walk 6 G1
Wilts Regiment Cotts...26 H1
Wiltshire Avenue 12 E1
Wiltshire Court*, Farnsby St.
..................................12 F3
Wimpole Close 10 G4
Winchcombe Close......10 F2
Winchester Close
   (Chippenham) 23 B1
Winchester Close (Swindon)
..................................7 D6
Windbrook Meadow 7 C3
Windermere 14 F6
Windflower Road 5 C2
Windlass Way...............24 F2
Windmill Court 10 G6
Windmill Piece 19 B5
Windrush 31 A3/A4/B3
Windrush Road.............. 6 E4
Windsor Close (Chippenham)
..................................23 B1
Windsor Close (Hook) ...9 A3
Windsor Drive 26 G3
Windsor Road................19 A1
Wine Street 25 D4
Wingate Parade 6 E5
Wingfield 7 C2
Wingfield Avenue 6 G1

Winifred Street 12 H6
Winlaw Close 11 A2
Winsley Close 6 G2
Winstanley Close 10 G5
Winters Court 35 A4
Winterslow Road 6 F2
Winton Close 36 H5
Winton Road 7 D3
Winwick Road 10 H5
Wirral Way 1 B6
Wise Close 7 A4
Wiseman Close 14 G3
Wishart Way 24 G2
Witfield Close 3 C2
Witham Way 7 B3
Withy Close 33 B2
Witts Lane 3 B2
Woburn Close 5 D1
Wolsely Avenue 13 B5
Wolverton Close 23 A1
Wood Hall Drive 5 B4
Wood Lane 22 F6/24 F1
Wood Road 13 C6
Wood Street (Calne)....29 B4
Wood Street (Swindon) 37 C6
Wood Street (Wootton B.)
..................................33 A3
Woodborough Road
   (Corsham) 35 D6
Woodborough Road
   (Pewsey) 34 E5
Woodbury Close 10 G1
Woodchester 11 A4
Woodcutters Mews 6 G1
Woodford Close 6 G1
Woodhill Avenue 29 C3
Woodhill Rise 29 C3
Woodhouse Road.........13 B4
Woodland Park............29 B5
Woodland View...........18 F2
Woodland Way ...25 D6/26 E6
Woodlands 35 A3
Woodlands Bungalows..21 C6
Woodlands Road
   (Chippenham) 21 C6
Woodlands Road
   (Marlborough) 28 H3
Woodlands Road
   (Pewsey) 34 G6
Woodpecker Mews......21 C3
Woodroffe Square 29 C4
Woodshaw Mead 33 D3
Woodside Avenue 13 A4
Woodside Road........8 E1/F1
Woodsman Road 6 F1
Woodspring Court 12 G6
Woodstock Road 8 E6
Woodward Court 37 B6
Woolford Grange 15 A1
Woollaton Close..........10 G4
Wootton Bassett Road ..11 C4
Wordsworth Close 33 C2
Wordsworth Drive 7 B3
Worlidge Drive 10 H1
Worsley Road......10 G5/G6
Wortheys Close 32 G2
Wrde Hill 31 B4
Wrenswood..................14 F2
Wright Close 1 B5
Wyatt Court 26 E6
Wychurch Road 32 G2
Wye House Gardens 28 E4
Wye House*,
   Wye House Gdns. 28 E4
Wylye Close 5 D3
Wylye Road 36 F5
Wynd, The 29 B3
Wyndham Close..........22 G5
Wyndham Road 12 E2
Wynndale Close 7 C3
Wynwards Road............6 E1
Wyvern Avenue 29 C4

Wyvern Close (Devizes)26 H1
Wyvern Close (Swindon)
..................................18 G1
Wyvern House 35 B5
Y
Yardley Close................5 D5
Yarmouth Close 10 H5
Yarnton Close 10 G1
Yarrow Close 5 A4
Yeats Close 1 C5
Yellowhammer Close*,
   Wagtail Close.....14 E1
Yeoman Close 10 G2
Yeovil Close 13 D4
Yew Tree Close*,
   Long Barrow Rd. .29 A4
Yew Tree Gardens.........8 G3
Yewstock Crescent East
..................................21 D4
Yewstock Crescent West
..................................21 D4
Yiewsley Crescent 7 D5
Yockney Close 35 C3
York Close (Chippenham)
..................................23 B1
York Close (Corsham) ..35 A4
York Place*, St. Martins 28 E4
York Road (Lyneham) ..34 H2
York Road (Swindon) ...37 C4
Z
Zoar Close 18 E5
Zouch Avenue 36 E3
Zouch Close 36 E4
Zouch Farm Road.........36 F4
Zouch Market 36 F3

ROUNDABOUTS
Akers Roundabout 5 B4
Blagrove Roundabout...10 F6
Bridge Mead Roundabout
..................................11 B3
Bruce Street Bridges 11 D1
Cockleberry Roundabout
..................................37 B1
Colbourne Roundabout 37 D1
Commonhead Roundabout
..................................20 G2
Cornbrash Park 21 B4
Cross Roundabout 10 H4
Deloro Roundabout 7 C4
Eastleaze Roundabout ..11 A3
Five Ways Roundabout 10 H3
Gablecross Roundabout..8 F5
Gainsborough Roundabout
..................................10 G4
Greenbridge Roundabout
..................................13 C1
Honda North Roundabout
..................................7 D2
Honda South Roundabout
..................................7 D3
Keypoint Roundabout......8 F5
Mannington Roundabout
..................................11 C4
Merlin Roundabout 14 F1
North Star Roundabout..12 F1
Oasis Roundabout 12 F1
Pipers Roundabout......19 A1
Priory Roundabout.......32 H5
Renault Roundabout 11 A2
The Magic Roundabout
..................13 A3/37 D3
The Meads Roundabout
..................................11 C3
Westlea Roundabout 11 A4
White Hart Roundabout ..8 F6
Whychurch Roundabout
..................................32 H2
Wills Roundabout 13 A1
Windmill Roundabout 10 F5
Withy Mead Roundabout
..................................11 A2

INDUSTRIAL ESTATES
Aspect Park 19 A1
Axis Business Centre 11 B2
Banda Ind. Estate 26 G5
Bath Road Business Centre
..................................25 A4
Bath Road Ind. Estate ..23 C1
Blackworth Ind. Estate ..31 C2
Blagrove Ind. Estate......16 G1
Britannia Ind. Estate......7 B5
Brunel Park..................21 A5
Bumpers Farm Ind. Estate
..................................21 B5
Calne Business Centre 29 C1
Central Trading Estate ..12 H6
Cheney Manor Ind. Estate
..................................5 C6
Chippenham Ind. Park ..24 H2
Cobham Centre 11 B2
Coped Hall Bus. Park...33 C2
Cornbrash Park 21 B4
Corsham Commercial Centre
..................................35 D4
Delta Business Park 11 B3/B4
Dorcan Business Village
..................................14 G3
Dorcan Complex, The ..14 G3
Dorcan Ind. Estate 14 G4
Dunbeath Trading Estate 7 A6
Elgin Industrial Estate......7 A5
Europa Industrial Park 7 B4
Euroway Ind. Park 16 F1
Fordbrook Ind. Estate ...34 F4
Four Brooks Bus. Park ..29 C1
Fraser Centre, The.......14 G3
Garden Trading Estate ..26 F2
Gipsy Lane Ind. Estate..13 A1
Gloucester Road Ind. Estate
..................................32 G3
Great Western Outlet Village
..................................12 E3
Greenbridge Ind. Estate
..................................13 B1/C1
Greenbridge Retail & Leisure
   Park 13 B1
Greenways Bus. Park....22 E3
Groundwell Ind. Estate....6 G1
Hathaway Retail Park....22 F5
Hawksworth Trading Estate
..................................12 E2
Headlands Trading Est. ..6 H4
Herman Miller Industrial Area
..................................23 C2
Hillmead Enterprise Park 4 G6
Honda Car Plant...........8 E3
Hopton Ind. Estate 26 G1
Interface Bus. Park.......33 D4
IO Centre 7 C4
Isis Trading Estate 13 B1
Ivy Lane Ind. Estate 22 E6
Kembrey Park...............7 A5
Kendrick Ind. Estate 11 C1
Kingsdown Ind. Estate....7 C1
Langley Park................ 22 G4
Lansdowne Court Bus. Centre
..................................21 B5
Lower Basset Down
   Workshops...........16 H5
Malmesbury Bus. Park ..32 F2
Mannington Retail Park 11 C5
Marshgate Ind. Estate ..13 B1
North Star Industrial Area
..................................12 F2
North Swindon District Centre
..................................5 C1
Nursteed Road Trading Est.
..................................26 F6
Okus Trading Estate....12 F6
Orbit Centre, The 11 C4
Park Lane Ind. Estate....35 C2
Parsonage Way Ind. Estate
..................................22 G3

Patheon Building 14 F3
Pipers Way Business Area
..................................18 H2
Pipsmore Park 21 A5
Portemarsh Ind. Estate 29 C1
Purton Industrial Estate ..3 B1
River Ray Industrial Estate
..................................11 C2
Rivermead Ind. Estate ..11 A1
Salisbury Road Bus. Park*,
   Salisbury Road....34 F6
South Marston Ind. Estate
..................................8 F1
St. Margaret's Retail Park
..................................8 F5
Station Industrial Estate 12 F2
Station Road Industrial Estate
..................................29 A5
Stratton Road Ind. Estate
..................................13 B1
Techno Trading Estate....6 H6
Templar's Way Ind. Estate
..................................33 B6
Tetbury Hill Ind. Estate ..32 F2
The Meads Business Centre
..................................11 C3
Thornhill Industrial Estate
..................................8 G4
Transfer Bridge Ind. Estate
..................................13 A1
Tyak Business Centre ...21 A5
Wakefield House 19 A1
West Swindon Centre ...10 H4
Westmead Ind. Estate ..11 B2
Westpoint Bus. Park.....21 B4
Windmill Hill Bus. Park .10 F6
Wroughton Bus. Park....18 G3